RAINER MARIA RILKE was born in Prague in 1875 and traveled through-out Europe for much of his adult life, returning frequently to Paris. There he came under the influence of the sculptor Auguste Rodin and produced much of his finest work, most notably the two volumes of *New Poems* as well as the great modernist novel *The Notebooks of Malte Laurids Brigge*. Among his other books of poems are *The Book of Images* and *The Book of Hours*. He lived the last years of his life in Switzerland, where he completed his two poetic masterworks, the *Duino Elegies* and *Sonnets to Orpheus*. He died of leukemia in December 1926.

EDWARD SNOW is a professor of English at Rice University. North Point Press has published his translations of Rilke's *New Poems [1907]*, *New Poems [1908]: The Other Part*, *The Book of Images*, and *Uncollected Poems*. He is the recipient of an Academy of Arts and Letters Award for the body of his Rilke translations, as well as the Academy of American Poets' Harold Morton Landon Translation Award and the PEN Award for Poetry in Translation. He is also the author of *A Study of Vermeer* and *Inside Bruegel*.

Duino Elegies

Duino Elegies

Rainer Maria Rilke

BILINGUAL EDITION

TRANSLATED BY *Edward Snow*

NORTH POINT PRESS

A DIVISION OF FARRAR, STRAUS AND GIROUX

NEW YORK

North Point Press
A division of Farrar, Straus and Giroux
18 West 18th Street, New York 10011

Copyright © 2000 by Edward Snow
Distributed in Canada by Douglas & McIntyre Ltd.
Printed in the United States of America
Published in 2000 by North Point Press
First paperback edition, 2001

The Library of Congress has cataloged the hardcover edition as follows:
Rilke, Rainer Maria, 1875–1926.
   [Duineser Elegien. English]
   Duino elegies : bilingual edition / Rainer Maria Rilke ; translated by Edward Snow.— 1st
      p.   cm.
   ISBN: 978-0-86547-546-5 (alk. paper)
   I. Title.   II. Snow, Edward A.

 PT2635.I65 D82 2000
 831'.912—dc21

                                                                                    99045

Paperback ISBN: 978-0-86547-607-3

Designed by Jonathan D. Lippincott

www.fsgbooks.com

15   14   13   12

CONTENTS

The *Duino Elegies* take their name from Castle Duino, an ancient fortress-like structure set high atop cliffs overlooking the Adriatic near Trieste. It was once a Roman watchtower, and Dante supposedly wrote parts of *The Divine Comedy* there. During the winter of 1911–12, Rainer Maria Rilke, feeling empty and despondent since completing *The Notebooks of Malte Laurids Brigge* in 1910, was residing there alone when the inspiration for the elegies came to him. Princess Marie von Thurn und Taxis-Hohenlohe (1855–1934), the friend and patron who made the castle available to him, relates in her memoir the story of their genesis:

> Rilke later told me how these elegies arose. He suspected nothing of what was taking hold inside him; though he may have hinted of it in a letter he wrote: "The nightingale is approaching—" Had he perhaps felt what was on its way? But things seemed again to fall silent. A great sadness came over him; he began to think that this winter too would be fruitless.
>
> Then, one morning, he received a troublesome business letter. He wanted to be done with it quickly, and had to concern himself with sums and other such tedious matters. Outside, a violent north wind was blowing, but the sun shone and the blue water had a silvery gleam. Rilke climbed down to the bastions which, jutting to the east and west, were connected to the foot of the castle by a narrow path along the cliffs. These cliffs fall steeply, for about two hundred feet, into the sea. Rilke paced back and forth, deep in thought, since the reply to the letter so concerned him. Then, all at once, in the midst of his brooding, he halted suddenly, for it seemed to him that in the raging of the storm a voice had called to him: "Who, if I cried out, would hear me among the angelic orders?" He stood still, listening. "What is that?" he half whispered. "What is it, what is coming?"
>
> He took out his notebook, which he always carried with him, and

wrote down these words, together with a few lines that formed them-
selves without his intervention. Who had come? And then he knew
the answer: the god . . .

Very calmly he climbed back up to his room, set his notebook
aside, and replied to the difficult letter.

By that evening the entire elegy had been written down.[1]

Rilke was elated; he copied the poem into a green leather-bound notebook
that he and the princess had bought together in Weimar and sent it to her in
Vienna on January 21 as "the first Duino work (and the first for a long
time!)." Within days he had composed the effortless-seeming "Second Elegy"
as well, along with fragments of the third, sixth, and ninth, and the opening
fifteen lines of the tenth. His task as a poet had been announced to him.

But nothing further would materialize at Duino. Rilke left the castle in
May with no more written, and recommenced the wanderings that had pre-
ceded his stay there. Though he continued to write brilliant poems in his
notebooks—150 in 1913 and 1914, several of them masterpieces—the *Elegies*
and his failure to sustain them were what obsessed him now.[2] ("Yes, the two
elegies exist," he wrote to his ex-lover and lifelong confidant Lou Andreas-
Salomé from Spain in January 1913, "but I can tell you when we meet how
small and sharply riven a fragment they form of what was then delivered into
my power.") During the next few years he would make sporadic progress: he
forced the uneven "Third Elegy" to completion in October 1913 in Paris, and
composed more lines of the sixth; in November 1915 he wrote the terse, ellip-
tical "Fourth Elegy" in just two days in Munich. But that would be all for
more than six years, until, in February 1922, in another castle-solitude in
Switzerland, the floodgates broke.

Rilke had been living alone since July 1921 in the Château de Muzot, a
small medieval tower in the Rhône valley near the village of Sierre, Switzer-
land, where he had deliberately isolated himself in hope of recapturing the in-
spiration of the elegies. ("I am now taking root and spinning a web around
myself inside a primeval tower . . . in the midst of this incomparably grand,
magnificent landscape," he wrote to Francisca Stoecklin on November 16.)
There, during three weeks in February, he experienced a creative storm so ex-

traordinary that his later mythologizing of the resulting work as "given" to him, a "dictation" for which he served as medium or scribe, is understandable. It began on February 2, when he unexpectedly began writing sonnets. After three days of uninterrupted work, he had produced twenty-five of the twenty-six poems that would form the first part of the *Sonnets to Orpheus*. On the morning of February 7, "The Seventh Elegy" came (all but the final lines, which he would add on February 26). That same day he began "The Eighth Elegy," the masterwork of the sequence, and finished it the following afternoon. On February 9, after completing "The Sixth Elegy," he composed the difficult ninth and all but the first four lines of "Antistrophes," a poem that would temporarily serve as the fifth. That evening he wrote excitedly to his publisher, Anton Kippenberg, that the *Elegies* were done ("My dear friend, I am over the mountain! The *Elegies* are here! . . . I went outside into the cold moonlight and stroked little Muzot like a big animal, its old walls which granted this to me . . . And my dear friend: *this*: that you have made this possible for me, have been so patient with me: *ten* years! Thanks! . . . And that you always believed in me—*thanks!*").

The next day was uneventful. Then, on February 11, Rilke returned to his draft of "The Tenth Elegy." He kept the first fifteen lines, which had existed since Duino, and composed a completely new version of the rest that same day (later, when asked, he would name the tenth as his favorite). He wrote at once to Princess Marie, who had remained for him, in an almost courtly sense, the patron of the *Elegies*:

At last,
                Princess,
At last, the blessed, *so* blessed day, when in this letter the conclusion—
so far as I see—of the
                                Elegies
                        I can announce to you:
                                TEN!
From the last, great one (with the opening begun back in Duino: "Someday, at the end of the nightmare of knowing, may I emerge singing praise and jubilation to assenting angels . . ."), from this last

one, which even then was intended to come last,—from this—my hand is still trembling! Just now, Saturday the eleventh, at six in the evening, it is finished!—

Everything in only a few days, it was an indescribable storm, a hurricane in my spirit (like that time in Duino), all the sinews and tissues in me groaned,—there was no thinking about food, God knows who fed me.

But now it is. Is. Is.

Amen.

So this is what I've survived for, through everything, on and on. Through Everything. All for this. *Only* this.

One of them I have dedicated to Kassner. But the whole is *yours*, Princess, how could it not be! Will be called:

The Duino Elegies

In the book there will be no dedication (for I can't give you what has been yours from the beginning) but instead:

From the property of . . .

That same evening Rilke wrote similar letters to Lou Andreas-Salomé and two other close friends—as if the accomplishing of the elegies, which required total solitude, was nonetheless a drama in which a whole circle of acquaintances had to be absorbed. Then, on February 14, in what Rilke described to Lou as a "radiant afterstorm," a final elegy came, the fifth, or "Saltimbanques," which he placed at the center of the cycle, discarding "Antistrophes," a poem that now felt to him inappropriate there.[3] With the *Elegies* complete (save for a handful of lines), there was a last surprise: the sonnets returned almost at once, and Rilke found himself writing nonstop again. Between February 15 and 23 he composed another cycle of twenty-nine fantastically experimental poems that would form the second part of the *Sonnets to Orpheus*.

After the second group of sonnets, the tempest at Muzot subsided, and Rilke's elation reached again toward friends. He copied out the last six elegies and sent them to Kippenberg on February 23, "for publication when he saw fit"; on the same day he sent the sonnets to Kippenberg's wife, Katharina (with whom he enjoyed a years-long friendship and correspondence), along with a separate letter asking her to judge if they were suitable for publication. (Both volumes were published sumptuously in 1923.) There was of course to be a copy for the Princess, but Rilke waited until she could visit him at Muzot, so that he could present the poems to her in person and read them to her aloud. That "great day" occurred on June 7. Princess Marie would remember it vividly:

> Secretive, tiny, low rooms with old furniture—flowers, many flowers everywhere, among them the five-petaled, flame-colored rose . . . We went up to the study—a room filled with books, filled with devotion. Adjacent to it the narrow bedroom and the little chapel . . . Everything seems as if created for the poet. And finally, standing at his desk as he always does, he began to read . . . As he read—wonderfully, as only he can read—I felt my heart beating more and more strongly, felt the tears running down my cheeks. There are no words for this experience. The next day—in the charming hotel room in Sierre—it was the sonnets' turn. Fifty-seven, and not one too many. Every word a jewel. Some of them make one's heart stand still.[4]

In July the Kippenbergs visited and again Rilke read—the *Elegies* one evening for the two of them, the sonnets the next morning for Katharina alone. Plans were discussed for the publication not only of the *Elegies* and the sonnets but of a five-volume edition of his complete works—so convinced was Rilke that all he had been given to say had been said.

In truth he would continue to write poems prolifically at Muzot—there are some thirty pieces in the notebooks from the latter months of 1923, and over a hundred poems in the notebooks of 1924, many of them among his finest. But Rilke never allowed any of this unpublished work to infiltrate his life's story as poet, which *had* to climax with the *Elegies*. (Even the sonnets he would think of as a "bonus" or "reward" that came with the *Elegies'* completion.) So many ethical evasions, disappointments, and things undone he had rationalized in terms of the "waiting" required of him by the task of the *Elegies,* that it was only by rehearsing the drama of their composition that he could feel himself justified and redeemed—even, albeit in a wishful sense, exemplary:

> That a man who had felt himself . . . cloven to his foundations [Rilke is looking back from December 1925, scarcely a year away from death, on how he was "saved" that February in Muzot] into a Formerly and an incompatible, dying Now: that such a man should experience the grace of being able to perceive how, in still more secret depths, *beneath* this torn-open cleft, the continuity of his work and of his mind was being restored . . . , seems to me more than a merely private occurrence; for by that token a measure is provided for the inexhaustible layering of our nature; and how many who, for one reason or another, believe they have been torn asunder, might not draw from this example of "continuability" their own particular consolation.
>
> (I would like to think that this consolation has also somehow become an aspect of the accomplishment of the great *Elegies,* so that they express themselves more completely than, without endangerment and rescue, could have been possible.)[5]

.

Despite Rilke's personal, sometimes almost hermetic investment in the elegies, he believed that his poetry spoke for itself. He distrusted commentaries as dilutions and foreclosures of the individual's reading experience. When a friend wrote to him that she felt the key to one of the *Sonnets to Orpheus* lay in the idea of the transmigration of souls, he responded: "You are thinking too far out beyond the poem itself . . . I believe that no poem in the *Sonnets to Orpheus* means anything that is not fully written out there, often, it is true, with its most secret name. All 'allusion' I am convinced would be contradictory to the indescribable 'being-there' of the poem."[6] In another context he wrote that his most recalcitrant obscurities may require not elucidation (*Aufklärung*) so much as "submitting-to" (*Unterwerfung*).[7] In this spirit I have held explanatory notes to a minimum: a few passages to give the flavor of Rilke's thinking, an occasional gloss on something perhaps now lost to us, and one attempt to address what may be a major misconception about "The Fifth Elegy." Since a guiding principle of this translation has been that it would be folly to ignore all the work that has already been done, I would like to express my debt to the following translators of all or parts of the elegies: J. B. Leishman and Stephen Spender, A. Poulin, Jr., Stephen Mitchell, Gary Miranda, David Young, C. F. MacIntyre, Stephen Cohn, David Oswald, Elaine E. Boney, Peter and Sheila Stern, Roger Paulin, William Gass, and Galway Kinnell. My thanks also to Michael Winkler, Jonathan Galassi, Paul Elie, Winifred Hamilton, and Ethan Nosowsky for their many helpful comments.

NOTES

1. Fürstin Marie von Thurn und Taxis-Hohenlohe, *Erinnerungen an Rainer Maria Rilke* (Munich and Berlin, 1932), pp. 40–41. Rilke and this remarkable woman twenty years his senior became intimate friends; she was arguably the most important *abiding* presence in the last fifteen years of his life. They corresponded about practically everything. (There are 120 letters from 1912 and 1913 alone: see *Briefwechsel mit Marie von Thurn und Taxis*, 2 vols., Frankfurt, 1986 [1951].) Here is Princess Marie answering, in a letter of March 9, 1913, one of Rilke's frequent "complaints":

Oh Dottor Serafico [her nickname for him], I envy you! I think you are the most fortunate man on God's earth (now you are getting mad as a bug—*con rispetto parlando*—but nevertheless it is true,—if only your remarkable eyes, which see everything with such extraordinary clarity, could see yourself as well). Very well, I will enumerate. You are a great poet, you know it perfectly well. You are in love (*don't* quibble, you *are* in love and always will be, where or with whom or for how long is beside the point). You have a small atelier in Paris—and it is March—the whole glorious spring is knocking at your door—Come in! I'm Dottor Serafico! Consider me—I'm a woman—and a woman my age should tear out every hair on her head every time she looks at herself in the mirror and then hang herself with the nearest rope. I have had so much trouble and worry in my life . . . And yet a blossoming fruit-tree and a golden sunbeam *make me wild with delight*! [in English in the original]. But, on the other hand, if you weren't so desperate you probably wouldn't write so wonderfully. So be desperate! Be really desperate, be even *more* desperate!

2. For a selection of the poems that remained uncollected in Rilke's notebooks and a discussion of the poet's curious neglect of that body of work, see *Rainer Maria Rilke: Uncollected Poems*, trans. Edward Snow (New York, 1996).

3. For the German text of "Antistrophes" and a translation, see *Rainer Marie Rilke: Uncollected Poems*, pp. 142–45. The poem is so different in style and voice from the other elegies that it is difficult to believe Rilke actually planned, until the last moment, to make it one of them. The forty-six-line poem praises women ("you") by contrasting them, in short counterpoised stanzas, to men ("we"):

> Childhood's breaking-off
> did you no harm. All at once
> you stood there, complete,
> as if made manifest in the god.

> We, as if broken from cliffs,
> even as young boys sharp
> at the edges, though sometimes
> perhaps smoothly cut;
> we, like large shards of stone
> dumped over flowers.

> Flowers of the deeper soil,
> loved by all roots,
> you, Eurydice's sisters,
> always full of sacred turning-back
> behind the ascending man.

4. *Erinnerungen*, pp. 93–94.

5. Letter to Arthur Fischer-Colbrie, December 18, 1925.

6. Letter to the Countess Sizzo, June 1, 1923, quoted and translated in Rilke, *Sonnets to Orpheus*, trans. M. D. Herder Norton (New York, 1943), pp. 10–11.

7. Letter to Clara Rilke, April 23, 1923.

Duino Elegies

DUINESER ELEGIEN

DUINO ELEGIES

FROM THE PROPERTY OF PRINCESS
MARIE VON THURN UND TAXIS-HOHENLOHE

Wer, wenn ich schriee, hörte mich denn aus der Engel
Ordnungen? und gesetzt selbst, es nähme
einer mich plötzlich ans Herz: ich verginge von seinem
stärkeren Dasein. Denn das Schöne ist nichts
als des Schrecklichen Anfang, den wir noch grade ertragen,
und wir bewundern es so, weil es gelassen verschmäht,
uns zu zerstören. Ein jeder Engel ist schrecklich.
   Und so verhalt ich mich denn und verschlucke den Lockruf
dunkelen Schluchzens. Ach, wen vermögen
wir denn zu brauchen? Engel nicht, Menschen nicht,
und die findigen Tiere merken es schon,
daß wir nicht sehr verläßlich zu Haus sind
in der gedeuteten Welt. Es bleibt uns vielleicht
irgend ein Baum an dem Abhang, daß wir ihn täglich
wiedersähen; es bleibt uns die Straße von gestern
und das verzogene Treusein einer Gewohnheit,
der es bei uns gefiel, und so blieb sie und ging nicht.
   O und die Nacht, die Nacht, wenn der Wind voller Weltraum
uns am Angesicht zehrt—, wem bliebe sie nicht, die ersehnte,
sanft enttäuschende, welche dem einzelnen Herzen
mühsam bevorsteht. Ist sie den Liebenden leichter?
Ach, sie verdecken sich nur mit einander ihr Los.
   Weißt du's *noch* nicht? Wirf aus den Armen die Leere
zu den Räumen hinzu, die wir atmen; vielleicht daß die Vögel
die erweiterte Luft fühlen mit innigerm Flug.

Ja, die Frühlinge brauchten dich wohl. Es muteten manche
Sterne dir zu, daß du sie spürtest. Es hob
sich eine Woge heran im Vergangenen, oder
da du vorüberkamst am geöffneten Fenster,

Who, if I cried out, would hear me among the angelic
orders? And even if one of them pressed me
suddenly to his heart: I'd be consumed
in his stronger existence. For beauty is nothing
but the beginning of terror, which we can just barely endure,
and we stand in awe of it as it coolly disdains
to destroy us. Every angel is terrifying.
    And so I check myself and swallow the luring call
of dark sobs. Alas, whom can we turn to
in our need? Not angels, not humans,
and the sly animals see at once
how little at home we are
in the interpreted world. That leaves us
some tree on a hillside, on which our eyes fasten
day after day; leaves us yesterday's street
and the coddled loyalty of an old habit
that liked it here, stayed on, and never left.
    O and the night, the night, when the wind full of worldspace
gnaws at our faces—, for whom *won't* the night be there,
desired, gently disappointing, a hard rendezvous
for each toiling heart. Is it easier for lovers?
Ah, but they only use each other to hide what awaits them.
    You still don't see? Cast the emptiness from your arms
into the spaces we breathe: perhaps the birds
will sense the increase of air with more passionate flying.

Yes, the springtimes needed you. Many a star was waiting
for your eyes only. A wave swelled toward you
out of the past, or a violin surrendered itself
as you walked by an open window. All that was mission.

gab eine Geige sich hin. Das alles war Auftrag.
Aber bewältigtest du's? Warst du nicht immer
noch von Erwartung zerstreut, als kündigte alles
eine Geliebte dir an? (Wo willst du sie bergen,
da doch die großen fremden Gedanken bei dir
aus und ein gehn und öfters bleiben bei Nacht.)
Sehnt es dich aber, so singe die Liebenden; lange
noch nicht unsterblich genug ist ihr berühmtes Gefühl.
Jene, du neidest sie fast, Verlassenen, die du
so viel liebender fandst als die Gestillten. Beginn
immer von neuem die nie zu erreichende Preisung;
denk: es erhält sich der Held, selbst der Untergang war ihm
nur ein Vorwand, zu sein: seine letzte Geburt.
Aber die Liebenden nimmt die erschöpfte Natur
in sich zurück, als wären nicht zweimal die Kräfte,
dieses zu leisten. Hast du der Gaspara Stampa
denn genügend gedacht, daß irgend ein Mädchen,
dem der Geliebte entging, am gesteigerten Beispiel
dieser Liebenden fühlt: daß ich würde wie sie?
Sollen nicht endlich uns diese ältesten Schmerzen
fruchtbarer werden? Ist es nicht Zeit, daß wir liebend
uns vom Geliebten befrein und es bebend bestehn:
wie der Pfeil die Sehne besteht, um gesammelt im Absprung
mehr zu sein als er selbst. Denn Bleiben ist nirgends.

Stimmen, Stimmen. Höre, mein Herz, wie sonst nur
Heilige hörten: daß sie der riesige Ruf
aufhob vom Boden; sie aber knieten,
Unmögliche, weiter und achtetens nicht:
So waren sie hörend. Nicht, daß du *Gottes* ertrügest
die Stimme, bei weitem. Aber das Wehende höre,
die ununterbrochene Nachricht, die aus Stille sich bildet.
Es rauscht jetzt von jenen jungen Toten zu dir.
Wo immer du eintratst, redete nicht in Kirchen
zu Rom und Neapel ruhig ihr Schicksal dich an?

But were you up to it? Weren't you always
distracted by expectation, as though each moment
announced a beloved's coming? (But where would you keep her,
with all those huge strange thoughts in you
going and coming and sometimes staying the night?)
No, in longing's grip sing women who *loved*:
their feats of passion still lack undying fame.
The bereft ones you almost envy, since you
found them so much bolder in love than those fulfilled.
To begin ever anew their impossible praise.
Remember: the hero lives on. Even his downfall
was only a pretext for attained existence, a final birth.
But nature, depleted, takes back into herself
women who loved, as though she lacked the strength
to create them a second time. Have you invoked Gaspara Stampa
enough so that any girl abandoned by her lover
would feel from this exalted model
of a woman's love: let me be as she was!
Isn't it time that these most ancient sorrows of ours
grew fruitful? Time that we tenderly loosed ourselves
from the loved one, and, unsteadily, survived:
the way the arrow, suddenly all vector, survives the string
to be more than itself. For abiding is nowhere.

Voices, voices. Listen, my heart, as before now
only saints had listened, while that vast call
raised them off the ground; yet they paid no heed
and kept on kneeling, those impossible ones,
listening wholly absorbed. Not that you could bear
God's voice—by no means. But listen to the wind's breathing,
that uninterrupted news that forms from silence.
It's rustling toward you now from all the youthful dead.
When you entered a church in Rome or Naples,
didn't their fate speak quietly to you?

Oder es trug eine Inschrift sich erhaben dir auf,
wie neulich die Tafel in Santa Maria Formosa.
Was sie mir wollen? leise soll ich des Unrechts
Anschein abtun, der ihrer Geister
reine Bewegung manchmal ein wenig behindert.

Freilich ist es seltsam, die Erde nicht mehr zu bewohnen,
kaum erlernte Gebräuche nicht mehr zu üben,
Rosen, und andern eigens versprechenden Dingen
nicht die Bedeutung menschlicher Zukunft zu geben;
das, was man war in unendlich ängstlichen Händen,
nicht mehr zu sein, und selbst den eigenen Namen
wegzulassen wie ein zerbrochenes Spielzeug.
Seltsam, die Wünsche nicht weiterzuwünschen. Seltsam,
alles, was sich bezog, so lose im Raume
flattern zu sehen. Und das Totsein ist mühsam
und voller Nachholn, daß man allmählich ein wenig
Ewigkeit spürt.—Aber Lebendige machen
alle den Fehler, daß sie zu stark unterscheiden.
Engel (sagt man) wüßten oft nicht, ob sie unter
Lebenden gehn oder Toten. Die ewige Strömung
reißt durch beide Bereiche alle Alter
immer mit sich und übertönt sie in beiden.

Schließlich brauchen sie uns nicht mehr, die Früheentrückten,
man entwöhnt sich des Irdischen sanft, wie man den Brüsten
milde der Mutter entwächst. Aber wir, die so große
Geheimnisse brauchen, denen aus Trauer so oft
seliger Fortschritt entspringt—: *könnten* wir sein ohne sie?
Ist die Sage umsonst, daß einst in der Klage um Linos
wagende erste Musik dürre Erstarrung durchdrang;
daß erst im erschrockenen Raum, dem ein beinah göttlicher Jüngling
plötzlich für immer enttrat, das Leere in jene
Schwingung geriet, die uns jetzt hinreißt und tröstet und hilft.

Or an inscription echoed deep inside you,
as, not long ago, that tablet in Santa Maria Formosa.
Their charge to me? —that I brush gently aside
the veil of injustice that sometimes
hinders a bit their spirits' pure movement.

True, it's strange to dwell on earth no longer,
to cease practicing customs barely learned,
not to give roses and other things of such promise
a meaning in some human future;
to stop being what one was in endlessly anxious hands,
and ignore even one's own name like a broken toy.
Strange, not to go on wishing one's wishes. Strange,
to see all that was once so interconnected
now floating in space. And death demands a labor,
a tying up of loose ends, before one has
that first feeling of eternity. —But the living
all make the same mistake: they distinguish too sharply.
Angels (it's said) often don't know whether they move among
the living or the dead. The eternal current
bears all the ages with it through both kingdoms
forever and drowns their voices in both.

In the end, those torn from us early no longer need us;
they grow slowly unaccustomed to earthly things, in the gentle manner
one outgrows a mother's breasts. But we, who need
such great mysteries, for whom so often blessed progress
springs from grief—: could *we* exist without *them*?
Is it a tale told in vain, that myth of lament for Linos,
in which music first pierced the shell of numbness:
shocked Space, which an almost divine youth
had suddenly left forever; then, in the void, vibrations—
which in us now are rapture and solace and help.

Jeder Engel ist schrecklich. Und dennoch, weh mir,
ansing ich euch, fast tödliche Vögel der Seele,
wissend um euch. Wohin sind die Tage Tobiae,
da der Strahlendsten einer stand an der einfachen Haustür,
zur Reise ein wenig verkleidet und schon nicht mehr furchtbar;
(Jüngling dem Jüngling, wie er neugierig hinaussah).
Träte der Erzengel jetzt, der gefährliche, hinter den Sternen
eines Schrittes nur nieder und herwärts: hochauf-
schlagend erschlüg uns das eigene Herz. Wer seid ihr?

Frühe Geglückte, ihr Verwöhnten der Schöpfung,
Höhenzüge, morgenrötliche Grate
aller Erschaffung,—Pollen der blühenden Gottheit,
Gelenke des Lichtes, Gänge, Treppen, Throne,
Räume aus Wesen, Schilde aus Wonne, Tumulte
stürmisch entzückten Gefühls und plötzlich, einzeln,
Spiegel: die die entströmte eigene Schönheit
wiederschöpfen zurück in das eigene Antlitz.

Denn wir, wo wir fühlen, verflüchtigen; ach wir
atmen uns aus und dahin; von Holzglut zu Holzglut
geben wir schwächern Geruch. Da sagt uns wohl einer:
ja, du gehst mir ins Blut, dieses Zimmer, der Frühling
füllt sich mit dir . . . Was hilfts, er kann uns nicht halten,
wir schwinden in ihm und um ihn. Und jene, die schön sind,
o wer hält sie zurück? Unaufhörlich steht Anschein
auf in ihrem Gesicht und geht fort. Wie Tau von dem Frühgras
hebt sich das Unsre von uns, wie die Hitze von einem
heißen Gericht. O Lächeln, wohin? O Aufschaun:
neue, warme, entgehende Welle des Herzens—;

Every angel is terrifying. And yet, alas,
I sing to you, almost fatal birds of the soul,
knowing what you are. Where are the days of Tobias,
when one of your most radiant stood at that simple doorway,
dressed for travel and no longer frightening
(to the youth who peered out curiously, a youth like him).
Were the archangel now to emerge from behind the stars
and take just one downward step this way:
our own thundering hearts would slay us. Who *are* you?

Favored first prodigies, creation's darlings,
mountain ranges, peaks, dawn-red ridges
of all genesis,—pollen of a flowering godhead,
links of light, corridors, stairs, thrones,
spaces of being, shields of rapture, torrents
of unchecked feeling and then suddenly, singly,
mirrors: scooping their outstreamed beauty
back into their peerless faces.

For our part, when we feel, we evaporate; ah, we breathe
ourselves out and away; with each new heartfire
we give off a fainter scent. True, someone may tell us:
you're in my blood, this room, Spring itself
is filled with you . . . To what end? He can't hold us,
we vanish within him and around him. And the beautiful ones,
ah, who holds *them* back? Appearance ceaselessly
flares in their faces and disappears. Like dew from the morning grass
what is ours rises from us, the way heat rises
from a steaming dish. O smile, going where? O upturned look:
new, warm, receding surge of the heart—;

weh mir: wir *sinds* doch. Schmeckt denn der Weltraum,
in den wir uns lösen, nach uns? Fangen die Engel
wirklich nur Ihriges auf, ihnen Entströmtes,
oder ist manchmal, wie aus Versehen, ein wenig
unseres Wesens dabei? Sind wir in ihre
Züge soviel nur gemischt wie das Vage in die Gesichter
schwangerer Frauen? Sie merken es nicht in dem Wirbel
ihrer Rückkehr zu sich. (Wie sollten sie's merken.)

Liebende könnten, verstünden sie's, in der Nachtluft
wunderlich reden. Denn es scheint, daß uns alles
verheimlicht. Siehe, die Bäume *sind*; die Häuser,
die wir bewohnen, bestehn noch. Wir nur
ziehen allem vorbei wie ein luftiger Austausch.
Und alles ist einig, uns zu verschweigen, halb als
Schande vielleicht und halb als unsägliche Hoffnung.

Liebende, euch, ihr in einander Genügten,
frag ich nach uns. Ihr greift euch. Habt ihr Beweise?
Seht, mir geschiehts, daß meine Hände einander
inne werden oder daß mein gebrauchtes
Gesicht in ihnen sich schont. Das giebt mir ein wenig
Empfindung. Doch wer wagte darum schon zu *sein*?
Ihr aber, die ihr im Entzücken des anderen
zunehmt, bis er euch überwältigt
anfleht: nicht *mehr*—; die ihr unter den Händen
euch reichlicher werdet wie Traubenjahre;
die ihr manchmal vergeht, nur weil der andre
ganz überhand nimmt: euch frag ich nach uns. Ich weiß,
ihr berührt euch so selig, weil die Liebkosung verhält,
weil die Stelle nicht schwindet, die ihr, Zärtliche,
zudeckt; weil ihr darunter das reine
Dauern verspürt. So versprecht ihr euch Ewigkeit fast
von der Umarmung. Und doch, wenn ihr der ersten

alas, we *are* that surge. Does then the cosmic space
we dissolve in taste of us? Do the angels
reclaim only what is theirs, their own outstreamed essence,
or sometimes, by accident, does a bit of us
get mixed in? Are we blended in their features
like the slight vagueness that complicates the looks
of pregnant women? Unnoticed by them in their
whirling back into themselves. (How *could* they notice?)

Lovers, if they only understood, might speak wondrously
in the night air. For everything, it seems,
seeks to conceal us. Look: the trees *exist*; the houses
we dwell in stand there stalwartly. Only we
pass by it all, like a rush of air.
And everything conspires to keep quiet about us,
half out of shame perhaps, half out of some secret hope.

You lovers, secure in one another, I ask you
about us. You hold each other. Have you assurances?
It sometimes happens that my hands
grow conscious of each other, or else my weary face
takes refuge in them. That gives me a slight
self-sensation. Yet who, from something so unwarranted,
would dare conclude, "I *am*"? You, though, who keep increasing
through the other's rapture, until, overwhelmed, each
begs the other: "No *more*"—; you who amid each other's hands
flourish like vines in vintage years;
you who disappear sometimes, only because the other
grows rampant; I ask you about us. I know
you touch so fervently because the caress preserves,
because the place you cover up, O tender ones,
doesn't disappear; because, underneath, you feel
pure permanence. Thus your embraces almost promise you
eternity. And yet, after you survive the terror

Blicke Schrecken besteht und die Sehnsucht am Fenster,
und den ersten gemeinsamen Gang, *ein* Mal durch den Garten:
Liebende, *seid* ihrs dann noch? Wenn ihr einer dem andern
euch an den Mund hebt und ansetzt—; Getränk an Getränk:
o wie entgeht dann der Trinkende seltsam der Handlung.

Erstaunte euch nicht auf attischen Stelen die Vorsicht
menschlicher Geste? war nicht Liebe und Abschied
so leicht auf die Schultern gelegt, als wär es aus anderm
Stoffe gemacht als bei uns? Gedenkt euch der Hände,
wie sie drucklos beruhen, obwohl in den Torsen die Kraft steht.
Diese Beherrschten wußten damit: so weit sind wirs,
dieses ist unser, uns *so* zu berühren; stärker
stemmen die Götter uns an. Doch dies ist Sache der Götter.

Fänden auch wir ein reines, verhaltenes, schmales
Menschliches, einen unseren Streifen Fruchtlands
zwischen Strom und Gestein. Denn das eigene Herz übersteigt uns
noch immer wie jene. Und wir können ihm nicht mehr
nachschaun in Bilder, die es besänftigen, noch in
göttliche Körper, in denen es größer sich mäßigt.

of the first look, and the long yearning at the window,
and that first walk—the one walk—together through the garden:
lovers, are you still the same? When you lift yourselves
each to the other's lips—drink unto drink:
O how strangely the drinker slips from the sacrament.

Remember those Attic stelae, how amazed you were at the caution
of human gestures; at the way love and parting were
laid so lightly on their shoulders, as if made of other stuff
than in our lives? And their hands, how they touched
without pressure, even though such power resides in the torsos.
Those self-mastered ones knew: we can go *this* far;
this much belongs to us, to touch each other *thus*; the gods
can grip us more forcefully. The choice is theirs.

If only we too could find some defined, narrow,
purely human place, our own small strip of fertile soil
between stream and stone. For even now our heart
transcends us, just as with those others. And no longer
can we gaze after it into pictures that soothe, or
into godlike bodies where it finds a grander restraint.

Eines ist, die Geliebte zu singen. Ein anderes, wehe,
jenen verborgenen schuldigen Fluß-Gott des Bluts.
Den sie von weitem erkennt, ihren Jüngling, was weiß er
selbst von dem Herren der Lust, der aus dem Einsamen oft,
ehe das Mädchen noch linderte, oft auch als wäre sie nicht,
ach, von welchem Unkenntlichen triefend, das Gotthaupt
aufhob, aufrufend die Nacht zu unendlichem Aufruhr.
O des Blutes Neptun, o sein furchtbarer Dreizack.
O der dunkele Wind seiner Brust aus gewundener Muschel.
Horch, wie die Nacht sich muldet und höhlt. Ihr Sterne,
stammt nicht von euch des Liebenden Lust zu dem Antlitz
seiner Geliebten? Hat er die innige Einsicht
in ihr reines Gesicht nicht aus dem reinen Gestirn?

Du nicht hast ihm, wehe, nicht seine Mutter
hat ihm die Bogen der Braun so zur Erwartung gespannt.
Nicht an dir, ihn fühlendes Mädchen, an dir nicht
bog seine Lippe sich zum fruchtbarern Ausdruck.
Meinst du wirklich, ihn hätte dein leichter Auftritt
also erschüttert, du, die wandelt wie Frühwind?
Zwar du erschrakst ihm das Herz; doch ältere Schrecken
stürzten in ihn bei dem berührenden Anstoß.
Ruf ihn . . . du rufst ihn nicht ganz aus dunkelem Umgang.
Freilich, er *will*, er entspringt; erleichtert gewöhnt er
sich in dein heimliches Herz und nimmt und beginnt sich.
Aber begann er sich je?
Mutter, *du* machtest ihn klein, du warsts, die ihn anfing;
dir war er neu, du beugtest über die neuen
Augen die freundliche Welt und wehrtest der fremden.
Wo, ach, hin sind die Jahre, da du ihm einfach

It's one thing to sing the loved one. Another, alas,
to sing that hidden guilty river-god of the blood!
Her youthful lover, whom she knows from afar: what sense has *he*
of that Lord of Lust who often, roused from solitude—
before she could soothe him, and often as though she herself
were nothing—ah, roused from what unsounded depths
lifts his streaming godhead, inciting the night to infinite uproar.
O the blood's Neptune, O his terrible trident.
O the dark wind of his breast from the shell's whorl.
Listen, as the night grows tunneled and cavelike. You stars,
does not the lover's delight in his beloved's face
come from you? Does not his passionate oneness with her pure
features derive from your celestial fire?

But not you, O girl, nor yet his mother,
stretched his eyebrows so fierce with expectation.
Not for your mouth, you who hold him now,
did his lips ripen into these fervent contours.
Do you really think your quiet footsteps
could have so convulsed him, you who move like dawn wind?
True, you startled his heart; but older terrors
rushed into him with that first jolt to his emotions.
Call him . . . you'll never quite retrieve him from those dark consorts.
Yes, he *wants* to, he escapes; relieved, he makes a home
in your familiar heart, takes root there and begins himself anew.
But did he *ever* begin himself?
Mother, *you* created him, you made him small;
with you he was new, and over his new eyes you arched
the friendly world, shutting the strange one out.
Where, *where* are those years, when with your slender form

mit der schlanken Gestalt wallendes Chaos vertratst?
Vieles verbargst du ihm so; das nächtlich-verdächtige Zimmer
machtest du harmlos, aus deinem Herzen voll Zuflucht
mischtest du menschlichern Raum seinem Nacht-Raum hinzu.
Nicht in die Finsternis, nein, in dein näheres Dasein
hast du das Nachtlicht gestellt, und es schien wie aus Freundschaft.
Nirgends ein Knistern, das du nicht lächelnd erklärtest,
so als wüßtest du längst, *wann* sich die Diele benimmt . . .
Und er horchte und linderte sich. So vieles vermochte
zärtlich dein Aufstehn; hinter den Schrank trat
hoch im Mantel sein Schicksal, und in die Falten des Vorhangs
paßte, die leicht sich verschob, seine unruhige Zukunft.

Und er selbst, wie er lag, der Erleichterte, unter
schläfernden Lidern deiner leichten Gestaltung
Süße lösend in den gekosteten Vorschlaf—:
schien ein Gehüteter . . . Aber *innen:* wer wehrte,
hinderte innen in ihm die Fluten der Herkunft?
Ach, da *war* keine Vorsicht im Schlafenden; schlafend,
aber träumend, aber in Fiebern: wie er sich ein-ließ.
Er, der Neue, Scheuende, wie er verstrickt war,
mit des innern Geschehns weiterschlagenden Ranken
schon zu Mustern verschlungen, zu würgendem Wachstum, zu tierhaft
jagenden Formen. Wie er sich hingab—. Liebte.
Liebte sein Inneres, seines Inneren Wildnis,
diesen Urwald in ihm, auf dessen stummem Gestürztsein
lichtgrün sein Herz stand. Liebte. Verließ es, ging die
eigenen Wurzeln hinaus in gewaltigen Ursprung,
wo seine kleine Geburt schon überlebt war. Liebend
stieg er hinab in das ältere Blut, in die Schluchten,
wo das Furchtbare lag, noch satt von den Vätern. Und jedes
Schreckliche kannte ihn, blinzelte, war wie verständigt.
Ja, das Entsetzliche lächelte . . . Selten
hast du so zärtlich gelächelt, Mutter. Wie sollte

you stood calmly between him and his surging chaos?
How much you kept from him that way; everything sinister
in his room at night you made harmless; from your heart's haven
you poured a more human space into his own shadowy world.
You placed the night-light not in the darkness
but in your nearer being, where it shone like a friend.
The slightest creak—and you explained it, smiling,
as though you'd long known just *when* the floor would act up . . .
And he listened and was soothed. Your quiet entrance
had such force; his tall, cloaked destiny
stepped behind the wardrobe, and his restless future,
gently shifting, molded itself to the folds of the curtain.

And he: lying there, calmed, beneath
drowsy eyelids the sweetness of your gentle presence
dissolving into the first hints of sleep—:
he *seemed* well-guarded. But *within*: who fended there,
who checked the floods of origin within him?
Ah, there *was* no caution in that sleeper; asleep,
but dreaming, and in a kind of fever: what paths he took!
He, so shy, so unwary, how embroiled he was,
with all those spreading tendrils of inner event already
twisted into primitive patterns, into throttling growth, into prowling
animal-like forms. How he gave in to it all—. Loved.
Loved his interior world, his secret jungle, that primeval
forest inside him, from whose floor of ancient downfall
his own heart rose, shimmering green. Loved it. Left it,
followed his roots into that violent source-world
where his small birth seemed all but nothing. Awestruck,
he descended into the elder blood, into the ravines
where things ghastly lay, still gorged with fathers. And every
Terror recognized him, winked, seemed to understand.
Yes, Horror smiled at him . . . Smiled
as seldom you smiled, mother. How could he not love

er es nicht lieben, da es ihm lächelte. *Vor* dir
hat ers geliebt, denn, da du ihn trugst schon,
war es im Wasser gelöst, das den Keimenden leicht macht.

Siehe, wir lieben nicht, wie die Blumen, aus einem
einzigen Jahr; uns steigt, wo wir lieben,
unvordenklicher Saft in die Arme. O Mädchen,
dies: daß wir liebten *in* uns, nicht Eines, ein Künftiges, sondern
das zahllos Brauende; nicht ein einzelnes Kind,
sondern die Väter, die wie Trümmer Gebirgs
uns im Grunde beruhn; sondern das trockene Flußbett
einstiger Mütter—; sondern die ganze
lautlose Landschaft unter dem wolkigen oder
reinen Verhängnis—: *dies* kam dir, Mädchen, zuvor.

Und du selber, was weißt du—, du locktest
Vorzeit empor in dem Liebenden. Welche Gefühle
wühlten herauf aus entwandelten Wesen. Welche
Frauen haßten dich da. Was für finstere Männer
regtest du auf im Geäder des Jünglings? Tote
Kinder wollten zu dir . . . O leise, leise,
tu ein liebes vor ihm, ein verläßliches Tagwerk,—führ ihn
nah an den Garten heran, gieb ihm der Nächte
Übergewicht . . . . . .
Verhalt ihn . . . . . .

what smiled at him that sweetly? He loved it
before you; for it was there even as you bore him,
dissolved in the fluid that carries the embryo.

You see, we don't love like flowers, the effort
of just one year; sap from time immemorial
flows through our arms when we love. O girl,
this: that we've loved, *within* us, not that one person yet to come,
but all the weltering brood; not some single child,
but the fathers who lie like mountain-ruins
within us; and the dried-up riverbed
of former mothers—; and the whole
soundless landscape beneath our cloudy
or cloudless fate: all *that*, O girl, claimed him first.

And you yourself, unwittingly—: you conjured
primal times in your lover. What feelings
writhed up out of beings long vanished! What
women inside him hated you! Who were those shrouded men
you raised in his youthful veins? Dead children
strained to reach you . . . O gently, gently,
show him the love that adheres to a calm, everyday task, —lead him
close to the garden, give him those nights
that even out the scales . . . . . .
                         Temper him . . . . . .

O Bäume Lebens, o wann winterlich?
Wir sind nicht einig. Sind nicht wie die Zug-
vögel verständigt. Überholt und spät,
so drängen wir uns plötzlich Winden auf
und fallen ein auf teilnahmslosen Teich.
Blühn und verdorrn ist uns zugleich bewußt.
Und irgendwo gehn Löwen noch und wissen,
solang sie herrlich sind, von keiner Ohnmacht.

Uns aber, wo wir Eines meinen, ganz,
ist schon des andern Aufwand fühlbar. Feindschaft
ist uns das Nächste. Treten Liebende
nicht immerfort an Ränder, eins im andern,
die sich versprachen Weite, Jagd und Heimat.
    Da wird für eines Augenblickes Zeichnung
ein Grund von Gegenteil bereitet, mühsam,
daß wir sie sähen; denn man ist sehr deutlich
mit uns. Wir kennen den Kontur
des Fühlens nicht: nur, was ihn formt von außen.
    Wer saß nicht bang vor seines Herzens Vorhang?
Der schlug sich auf: die Szenerie war Abschied.
Leicht zu verstehen. Der bekannte Garten,
und schwankte leise: dann erst kam der Tänzer.
Nicht *der*. Genug! Und wenn er auch so leicht tut,
er ist verkleidet und er wird ein Bürger
und geht durch seine Küche in die Wohnung.
    Ich will nicht diese halbgefüllten Masken,
lieber die Puppe. Die ist voll. Ich will
den Balg aushalten und den Draht und ihr
Gesicht aus Aussehn. Hier. Ich bin davor.

O trees of life, how far off is winter?
We're in disarray. Our minds don't commune
like those of migratory birds. Left behind and late,
we force ourselves suddenly on winds
and fall, exhausted, on indifferent waters.
Blooming makes us think of fading.
And somewhere out there lions still roam, oblivious,
in all their splendor, to any weakness.

We, though, even when intent on one thing wholly,
already feel the cost exacted by some other. Conflict
is our next of kin. Aren't lovers always
reaching borders, each in the other,
despite the promise of vastness, royal hunting, home?
        Then: for an instant's virtuoso sketch
a ground of contrast is prepared, laboriously,
so we can see it; for they're very clear
with us. We don't know our feelings' contour,
only what shapes it from outside.
        Who hasn't sat anxiously before his heart's curtain?
It rose: the scenery for *Parting*.
Easy to understand. The familiar garden,
swaying slightly: then—the dancer.
Not *him*. Enough! However light his entrance
he's in disguise and turns into a burgher
who enters his kitchen to reach his living room.
        I loathe watching these half-filled masks;
give me the puppet. At least it's real. I can take
the hollow body and the wire and the face
that is pure surface. Right here. I'm out in front.

Wenn auch die Lampen ausgehn, wenn mir auch
gesagt wird: Nichts mehr—, wenn auch von der Bühne
das Leere herkommt mit dem grauen Luftzug,
wenn auch von meinen stillen Vorfahrn keiner
mehr mit mir dasitzt, keine Frau, sogar
der Knabe nicht mehr mit dem braunen Schielaug:
Ich bleibe dennoch. Es giebt immer Zuschaun.

Hab ich nicht recht? Du, der um mich so bitter
das Leben schmeckte, meines kostend, Vater,
den ersten trüben Aufguß meines Müssens,
da ich heranwuchs, immer wieder kostend
und, mit dem Nachgeschmack so fremder Zukunft
beschäftigt, prüftest mein beschlagnes Aufschaun,—
der du, mein Vater, seit du tot bist, oft
in meiner Hoffnung, innen in mir, Angst hast,
und Gleichmut, wie ihn Tote haben, Reiche
von Gleichmut, aufgiebst für mein bißchen Schicksal,
hab ich nicht recht? Und ihr, hab ich nicht recht,
die ihr mich liebtet für den kleinen Anfang
Liebe zu euch, von dem ich immer abkam,
weil mir der Raum in eurem Angesicht,
da ich ihn liebte, überging in Weltraum,
in dem ihr nicht mehr wart . . . . : wenn mir zumut ist,
zu warten vor der Puppenbühne, nein,
so völlig hinzuschaun, daß, um mein Schauen
am Ende aufzuwiegen, dort als Spieler
ein Engel hinmuß, der die Bälge hochreißt.
Engel und Puppe: dann ist endlich Schauspiel.
Dann kommt zusammen, was wir immerfort
entzwein, indem wir da sind. Dann entsteht
aus unsern Jahreszeiten erst der Umkreis
des ganzen Wandelns. Über uns hinüber
spielt dann der Engel. Sieh, die Sterbenden,

Even when the lights go out, even when someone
says to me: "It's over—," even when from the stage
a gray gust of emptiness drifts toward me,
even when not one silent ancestor
sits beside me anymore—not a woman, not even
the boy with the brown squint-eye:
I'll sit here anyway. One can always watch.

Aren't I right? You, father, for whom life
turned so bitter when you tasted mine—
that first murky influx of what would feed my drives—
who kept on sampling it as I grew older, and,
intrigued by the aftertaste of so strange a future,
tried looking through my vague upward gaze,—
you, father, who since your death have been here
often in my hope, far inside me, afraid,
forfeiting that equanimity the dead possess, whole
kingdoms of equanimity, for my bit of fate—
Aren't I right? And you women—aren't I right?—
who loved me for that small, hesitating
love for you I always veered from,
because I felt the realm in your faces, even
as I loved it, changing into worldspace
where you were absent . . . : what if I do choose
to wait in front of the puppet stage—no,
to *stare* with so much force that finally, to counteract
my stare, an Angel will arrive here as an actor,
and jolt life into those hard husks.
Angel and Puppet: then, finally, the play begins.
Then what we keep apart, simply by our
presence here, conjoins. Then from the separate
seasons of our life that one great wheel
of transformation arises. Above us, beyond us,
the angel plays. The dying—surely *they*

sollten sie nicht vermuten, wie voll Vorwand
das alles ist, was wir hier leisten. Alles
ist nicht es selbst. O Stunden in der Kindheit,
da hinter den Figuren mehr als nur
Vergangnes war und vor uns nicht die Zukunft.
Wir wuchsen freilich und wir drängten manchmal,
bald groß zu werden, denen halb zulieb,
die andres nicht mehr hatten, als das Großsein.
Und waren doch, in unserem Alleingehn,
mit Dauerndem vergnügt und standen da
im Zwischenraume zwischen Welt und Spielzeug,
an einer Stelle, die seit Anbeginn
gegründet war für einen reinen Vorgang.

Wer zeigt ein Kind, so wie es steht? Wer stellt
es ins Gestirn und giebt das Maß des Abstands
ihm in die Hand? Wer macht den Kindertod
aus grauem Brot, das hart wird,—oder läßt
ihn drin im runden Mund, so wie den Gröps
von einem schönen Apfel? . . . . . . Mörder sind
leicht einzusehen. Aber dies: den Tod,
den ganzen Tod, noch *vor* dem Leben so
sanft zu enthalten und nicht bös zu sein,
ist unbeschreiblich.

must guess how full of pretext
is all that we achieve here. Nothing
is what it is. O childhood hours,
when behind each shape there was more
than mere past, and before us—not the future.
True, we were growing, and often we spurred ourselves
to grow up faster, half for the sake of those
who had nothing left but their grownness.
And yet, off alone, we were happy
with what stayed the same, and we stood there
in the space between world and plaything,
upon a spot which, from the first beginning,
had been established for pure event.

Who shows a child just as he is? Who places him
in a constellation and hands him the measure
of distance and interval? Who makes a child's death
out of gray bread that hardens,—or leaves
it in his round mouth like the core
of a beautiful apple? . . . . . . Murderers are
easily understood. But this: one's death,
the whole reach of death, even before one's life is under way,—
to hold it gently and not feel anger:
is indescribable.

Frau Hertha Koenig zugeeignet

Wer aber *sind* sie, sag mir, die Fahrenden, diese ein wenig
Flüchtigern noch als wir selbst, die dringend von früh an
wringt ein *wem, wem* zu Liebe
niemals zufriedener Wille? Sondern er wringt sie,
biegt sie, schlingt sie und schwingt sie,
wirft sie und fängt sie zurück; wie aus geölter,
glatterer Luft kommen sie nieder
auf dem verzehrten, von ihrem ewigen
Aufsprung dünneren Teppich, diesem verlorenen
Teppich im Weltall.
Aufgelegt wie ein Pflaster, als hätte der Vorstadt-
Himmel der Erde dort wehe getan.
                                    Und kaum dort,
aufrecht, da und gezeigt: des Dastehns
großer Anfangsbuchstab . . . , schon auch, die stärksten
Männer, rollt sie wieder, zum Scherz, der immer
kommende Griff, wie August der Starke bei Tisch
einen zinnenen Teller.

Ach und um diese
Mitte, die Rose des Zuschauns:
blüht und entblättert. Um diesen
Stampfer, den Stempel, den von dem eignen
blühenden Staub getroffnen, zur Scheinfrucht
wieder der Unlust befruchteten, ihrer
niemals bewußten,—glänzend mit dünnster
Oberfläche leicht scheinlächelnden Unlust.

Da: der welke, faltige Stemmer,
der alte, der nur noch trommelt,

THE FIFTH ELEGY

Dedicated to Frau Hertha Koenig

But tell me, who *are* they, these wanderers
(more rootless even than we ourselves) seized early on
and urgently wrung—for whose *possible* sake?—
by some never satisfied will. And still it wrings them,
bends them, twists them and slings them,
tosses and catches them; as if through smooth,
frictionless air they drop down
onto the threadbare carpet worn ever thinner
by their eternal leaping, this carpet
lost in the universe.
Laid down like a bandage, as if the jagged
sky of the city's edges had wounded the earth there.
                              And scarcely there,
erected, held on display: that first capital letter
from their bodies' alphabet . . . , when already the Grip
returns, rolling them up again, even the strongest
men, as if in some jest, like August the Strong at his table
curling pewter plates.

Ah, and around this
core, the rose of onlooking—
blooming and shedding petals. Around this
pestle, this pistil dusted
by its own pollen, impregnated once more
to bear the fake fruit of boredom—
boredom self-concealed
beneath the thinnest glaze of fake smiling.

There: the withered Strongman, his skin all folds,
the old one, who only drums now,

eingegangen in seiner gewaltigen Haut, als hätte sie früher
ʒwei Männer enthalten, und einer
läge nun schon auf dem Kirchhof, und er überlebte den andern,
taub und manchmal ein wenig
wirr, in der verwitweten Haut.

Aber der junge, der Mann, als wär er der Sohn eines Nackens
und einer Nonne: prall und strammig erfüllt
mit Muskeln und Einfalt.

Oh ihr,
die ein Leid, das noch klein war,
einst als Spielzeug bekam, in einer seiner
langen Genesungen . . . .

Du, der mit dem Aufschlag,
wie nur Früchte ihn kennen, unreif,
täglich hundertmal abfällt vom Baum der gemeinsam
erbauten Bewegung (der, rascher als Wasser, in wenig
Minuten Lenz, Sommer und Herbst hat)—
abfällt und anprallt ans Grab:
manchmal, in halber Pause, will dir ein liebes
Antlitz entstehn hinüber zu deiner selten
zärtlichen Mutter; doch an deinen Körper verliert sich,
der es flächig verbraucht, das schüchtern
kaum versuchte Gesicht . . . Und wieder
klatscht der Mann in die Hand zu dem Ansprung, und eh dir
jemals ein Schmerz deutlicher wird in der Nähe des immer
trabenden Herzens, kommt das Brennen der Fußsohln
ihm, seinem Ursprung, zuvor mit ein paar dir
rasch in die Augen gejagten leiblichen Tränen.
Und dennoch, blindlings,
das Lächeln . . . . .

shriveled up inside his great physique, as though
it once held *two* men, and now one
lies dead in the churchyard, and he survived that other,
deaf, and sometimes a bit confused
in the widowed skin.

But there the young one, the man in full, who might be the offspring
of a neck and a nun: strapping and stretched taut
with sinews and simpleness.

Oh and you,
once given as a plaything
to a young Grief, something to entertain it
during one of its long convalescences . . .

And you, who with a thud
that only unripe fruit knows
fall a hundred times daily from that tree
of mutually built motion (a tree swifter than water, traversing
spring, summer, autumn in a few moments):
fall and knock against the grave:
sometimes, during a brief pause, a tender look
edges forward to bridge the chasm
to your remote mother; but it gets lost on your body,
whose surface quickly assimilates that shy,
scarcely attempted face . . . And again
the man claps his hands for the leap, but before
a pain can enter the chambers of your
ever-racing heart and define itself there,
the burning in the soles of your feet intercepts it,
chasing into your eyes a few bodily tears.
And once again, blindly,
the smile . . . . .

Engel! o nimms, pflücks, das kleinblütige Heilkraut.
Schaff eine Vase, verwahrs! Stells unter jene, uns *noch* nicht
offenen Freuden; in lieblicher Urne
rühms mit blumiger schwungiger Aufschrift: ›*Subrisio Saltat.*‹

Du dann, Liebliche,
du, von den reizendsten Freuden
stumm Übersprungne. Vielleicht sind
deine Fransen glücklich für dich—,
oder über den jungen
prallen Brüsten die grüne metallene Seide
fühlt sich unendlich verwöhnt und entbehrt nichts.
Du,
immerfort anders auf alle des Gleichgewichts schwankende Waagen
hingelegte Marktfrucht des Gleichmuts,
öffentlich unter den Schultern.

Wo, o *wo* ist der Ort—ich trag ihn im Herzen—,
wo sie noch lange nicht *konnten*, noch von einander
abfieln, wie sich bespringende, nicht recht
paarige Tiere;—
wo die Gewichte noch schwer sind;
wo noch von ihren vergeblich
wirbelnden Stäben die Teller
torkeln . . . . .

Und plötzlich in diesem mühsamen Nirgends, plötzlich
die unsägliche Stelle, wo sich das reine Zuwenig
unbegreiflich verwandelt—, umspringt
in jenes leere Zuviel.
Wo die vielstellige Rechnung
zahlenlos aufgeht.

Plätze, o Platz in Paris, unendlicher Schauplatz,
wo die Modistin, *Madame Lamort,*

Angel! O take it, pluck it, that small-petaled herb of healing!
Create a vase, preserve it! Place it among those joys
not yet open to us; in a delicate urn
let an ornate inscription praise it: *"Subrisio Saltat."*

Then you, my sweetest,
you, whom the most ravishing joys
leapt over soundlessly.
Perhaps your fringes feel happy *for* you—,
or the green metallic silk
that covers your firm young breasts
feels endlessly pampered and wants for nothing.
You,
market-fruit of equanimity, forever repositioned
on the scales of a wavering equipoise,
a public thing among shoulders.

Where, *where* is that place—I carry it in my heart—
where for so long they still could *not*, still fell away
from each other like mismatched animals
trying to mate;—
where the weights are still heavy;
where the plates still topple
from the sticks that twirl and twirl
in vain . . . . .

And then, in this laborious nowhere,
suddenly the ineffable point where the pure too-little
mysteriously reverses—, flips round into
that empty too-much.
Where the complex equation
equals zero.

Squares, O town-square in Paris, infinite showplace
where the *modiste* Madame Lamort

die ruhlosen Wege der Erde, endlose Bänder,
schlingt und windet und neue aus ihnen
Schleifen erfindet, Rüschen, Blumen, Kokarden, künstliche Früchte——, alle
unwahr gefärbt,—für die billigen
Winterhüte des Schicksals.
. . . .

Engel! : Es wäre ein Platz, den wir nicht wissen, und dorten,
auf unsäglichem Teppich, zeigten die Liebenden, die's hier
bis zum Können nie bringen, ihre kühnen
hohen Figuren des Herzschwungs,
ihre Türme aus Lust, ihre
längst, wo Boden nie war, nur an einander
lehnenden Leitern, bebend,—und *könntens*,
vor den Zuschauern rings, unzähligen lautlosen Toten:
    Würfen die dann ihre letzten, immer ersparten,
immer verborgenen, die wir nicht kennen, ewig
gültigen Münzen des Glücks vor das endlich
wahrhaft lächelnde Paar auf gestilltem
Teppich?

weaves and winds the restless roads of the earth—
endless ribbons—designing new bows,
faddish frills, flowers, cockades, artificial fruit,
all falsely dyed, to adorn
the cheap winter hats of fate.
. . . .

Angel! Suppose there's a place we don't know of, and there,
on an indescribable carpet, lovers announced
those feats that they never mastered here—the bold, high
figures of their heartleaps through space,
their towers of pure pleasure, their two ladders
that stand leaning only against each other
with no ground underneath, trembling, —and then *performed* them,
before the circle of onlookers, the innumerable silent dead:
   Would not those dead throw their last coins
of happiness—hoarded through a lifetime,
kept hidden through a lifetime, unknown to us, eternally
valid—onto the blissful carpet before a pair
now *truly* smiling at last?

DIE SECHSTE ELEGIE

Feigenbaum, seit wie lange schon ists mir bedeutend,
wie du die Blüte beinah ganz überschlägst
und hinein in die zeitig entschlossene Frucht,
ungerühmt, drängst dein reines Geheimnis.
Wie der Fontäne Rohr treibt dein gebognes Gezweig
abwärts den Saft und hinan: und er springt aus dem Schlaf,
fast nicht erwachend, ins Glück seiner süßesten Leistung.
Sieh: wie der Gott in den Schwan.

...... Wir aber verweilen,
ach, uns rühmt es zu blühn, und ins verspätete Innre
unserer endlichen Frucht gehn wir verraten hinein.
Wenigen steigt so stark der Andrang des Handelns,
daß sie schon anstehn und glühn in der Fülle des Herzens,
wenn die Verführung zum Blühn wie gelinderte Nachtluft
ihnen die Jugend des Munds, ihnen die Lider berührt:
Helden vielleicht und den frühe Hinüberbestimmten,
denen der gärtnernde Tod anders die Adern verbiegt.
Diese stürzen dahin: dem eigenen Lächeln
sind sie voran, wie das Rossegespann in den milden
muldigen Bildern von Karnak dem siegenden König.

Wunderlich nah ist der Held doch den jugendlich Toten. Dauern
ficht ihn nicht an. Sein Aufgang ist Dasein; beständig
nimmt er sich fort und tritt ins veränderte Sternbild
seiner steten Gefahr. Dort fänden ihn wenige. Aber,
das uns finster verschweigt, das plötzlich begeisterte Schicksal
singt ihn hinein in den Sturm seiner aufrauschenden Welt.
Hör ich doch keinen wie *ihn*. Auf einmal durchgeht mich
mit der strömenden Luft sein verdunkelter Ton.

O fig tree, how long I've pondered you—
the way you almost skip flowering completely
and release, unheralded, your pure secret
into the sprigs of fruit already poised to ripen.
Like a fountain's pipe, your bent boughs drive the sap
downward and up: and it leaps from sleep, almost
without waking, into the joy of its sweetest achievement.
Look: like the god into the swan.

      . . . . . . But we, for our part, linger,
ah, flowering flatters us; the belated inner place
that is our culminating fruit we enter spent, betrayed.
Only a few feel the sap of action rise so strongly
that they're stationed and glowing in their heart's fullness
by the time the allure of flowering touches their eyelids,
touches their lips' youthfulness, like soft nocturnal air—
heroes perhaps, and those destined to leave early,
whose veins gardener Death twists in a different fashion.
These plunge on, in advance of their own smiles,
the way those teams of chargers precede the conquering
kings in the gentle bas-reliefs at Karnak.

Oddly, the hero resembles the youthful dead. Permanence
does not concern him. *Ascent* is his existence; time and again
he annuls himself and enters the changed constellation
of his unchanging danger. Few would find him there. But Fate,
which wraps us in mute obscurity, grows ecstatic
and sings him into the storms of his tumultuous world.
I hear no one like *him*. But suddenly I'm pierced
by his darkened music, borne swiftly by the rush of air.

Dann, wie verbärg ich mich gern vor der Sehnsucht: O wär ich,
wär ich ein Knabe und dürft es noch werden und säße
in die künftigen Arme gestützt und läse von Simson,
wie seine Mutter erst nichts und dann alles gebar.

War er nicht Held schon in dir, o Mutter, begann nicht
dort schon, in dir, seine herrische Auswahl?
Tausende brauten im Schooß und wollten *er* sein,
aber sieh: er ergriff und ließ aus—, wählte und konnte.
Und wenn er Säulen zerstieß, so wars, da er ausbrach
aus der Welt deines Leibs in die engere Welt, wo er weiter
wählte und konnte. O Mütter der Helden, o Ursprung
reißender Ströme! Ihr Schluchten, in die sich
hoch von dem Herzrand, klagend,
schon die Mädchen gestürzt, künftig die Opfer dem Sohn.

Denn hinstürmte der Held durch Aufenthalte der Liebe,
jeder hob ihn hinaus, jeder ihn meinende Herzschlag,
abgewendet schon, stand er am Ende der Lächeln,
                                        —anders.

Then how gladly I would hide from that longing! If only,
oh if only I were a boy with the unknown yet before me
as I sat propped on my future's arms, reading about Samson,
how his mother bore nothing at first, then—everything.

Was he not always the hero, O mother, even in you?
Did it not already begin there in you, his imperious choosing?
Thousands teemed in the womb, wanting to be *him*,
but look: he seized and excluded—, chose and made good.
If he crushed columns, it was when he burst
from the world of your body into the narrower world,
where he continued to choose and make good. O mothers of heroes,
O source of torrential rivers! You ravines into which,
high on the heart's rim, lamenting virgins
have cast themselves, lives-to-be sacrificed to the son.

For even as the hero stormed through love's arbors,
each heartbeat meant for him bore him upward and on: until
turned away already, he stood at the end of the smiles,
                                            —someone new.

Werbung nicht mehr, nicht Werbung, entwachsene Stimme,
sei deines Schreies Natur; zwar schrieest du rein wie der Vogel,
wenn ihn die Jahreszeit aufhebt, die steigende, beinah vergessend,
daß er ein kümmerndes Tier und nicht nur ein einzelnes Herz sei,
das sie ins Heitere wirft, in die innigen Himmel. Wie er, so
würbest du wohl, nicht minder—, daß, noch unsichtbar,
dich die Freundin erführ, die stille, in der eine Antwort
langsam erwacht und über dem Hören sich anwärmt,—
deinem erkühnten Gefühl die erglühte Gefühlin.

O und der Frühling begriffe—, da ist keine Stelle,
die nicht trüge den Ton der Verkündigung. Erst jenen kleinen
fragenden Auflaut, den, mit steigernder Stille,
weithin umschweigt ein reiner bejahender Tag.
Dann die Stufen hinan, Ruf-Stufen hinan, zum geträumten
Tempel der Zukunft—; dann den Triller, Fontäne,
die zu dem drängenden Strahl schon das Fallen zuvornimmt
im versprechlichen Spiel . . . . Und vor sich, den Sommer.

Nicht nur die Morgen alle des Sommers—, nicht nur
wie sie sich wandeln in Tag und strahlen vor Anfang.
Nicht nur die Tage, die zart sind um Blumen, und oben,
um die gestalteten Bäume, stark und gewaltig.
Nicht nur die Andacht dieser entfalteten Kräfte,
nicht nur die Wege, nicht nur die Wiesen im Abend,
nicht nur, nach spätem Gewitter, das atmende Klarsein,
nicht nur der nahende Schlaf und ein Ahnen, abends . . .
sondern die Nächte! Sondern die hohen, des Sommers,
Nächte, sondern die Sterne, die Sterne der Erde.
O einst tot sein und sie wissen unendlich,
alle die Sterne: denn wie, wie, wie sie vergessen!

No longer, voice. No longer let wooing send forth your cry:
you're past that. Even though your cry would be clear as a bird's
when first Spring bears him aloft, almost forgetting
that he's a cautious creature and not an unsheathed heart
being flung into brightness, into passionate skies.
Like him, with all his art, you'd also woo—: invisibly,
so that some silent mate might learn of you, and,
as she listened, a reply would slowly wake and grow warm—
the kindled complement of your own ardent feeling.

O and Spring would understand—, annunciation
would echo everywhere. First those small
questioning notes, which a clear, confident day
would surround with heightening silence.
Then up the calls, up that long flight of steps to the dreamt-of
temple of the future—; then the trill, that fountain,
whose urgent jet is teased by its falling
where promise is foreplay . . . And on ahead, the summer.

Not only all of summer's dawns—, not only
how they change into day and gleam with genesis.
Not only the days, so tender around flowers, and above,
in the patterned treetops, so forceful and strong.
Not only the calm reverence in these outspread powers,
not only the paths, the meadows as evening deepens,
not only, after late thunderstorms, the pulsing clarity,
not only the onset of sleep and, near dusk, a premonition . . .
But the nights! Those towering summer
nights! And the stars, the stars of the earth!
O to be dead and to know them endlessly,
all the stars: for how, how, how to forget them!

Siehe, da rief ich die Liebende. Aber nicht *sie* nur
käme . . . Es kämen aus schwächlichen Gräbern
Mädchen und ständen . . . Denn, wie beschränk ich,
wie, den gerufenen Ruf? Die Versunkenen suchen
immer noch Erde.—Ihr Kinder, ein hiesig
einmal ergriffenes Ding gälte für viele.
Glaubt nicht, Schicksal sei mehr, als das Dichte der Kindheit;
wie überholtet ihr oft den Geliebten, atmend,
atmend nach seligem Lauf, auf nichts zu, ins Freie.

Hiersein ist herrlich. Ihr wußtet es, Mädchen, *ihr* auch,
die ihr scheinbar entbehrtet, versankt—, ihr, in den ärgsten
Gassen der Städte, Schwärende, oder dem Abfall
Offene. Denn eine Stunde war jeder, vielleicht nicht
ganz eine Stunde, ein mit den Maßen der Zeit kaum
Meßliches zwischen zwei Weilen—, da sie ein Dasein
hatte. Alles. Die Adern voll Dasein.
Nur, wir vergessen so leicht, was der lachende Nachbar
uns nicht bestätigt oder beneidet. Sichtbar
wollen wirs heben, wo doch das sichtbarste Glück uns
erst zu erkennen sich giebt, wenn wir es innen verwandeln.

Nirgends, Geliebte, wird Welt sein, als innen. Unser
Leben geht hin mit Verwandlung. Und immer geringer
schwindet das Außen. Wo einmal ein dauerndes Haus war,
schlägt sich erdachtes Gebild vor, quer, zu Erdenklichem
völlig gehörig, als ständ es noch ganz im Gehirne.
Weite Speicher der Kraft schafft sich der Zeitgeist, gestaltlos
wie der spannende Drang, den er aus allem gewinnt.
Tempel kennt er nicht mehr. Diese, des Herzens, Verschwendung
sparen wir heimlicher ein. Ja, wo noch eins übersteht,
ein einst gebetetes Ding, ein gedientes, gekniertes—,
hält es sich, so wie es ist, schon ins Unsichtbare hin.
Viele gewahrens nicht mehr, doch ohne den Vorteil,
daß sie's nun *innerlich* baun, mit Pfeilern und Statuen, größer!

And thus: I'd call my lover. But not only *she*
would come . . . Other girls would come from crumbling graves
and stand before me . . . For could I limit
my call to just one? The interred seek
the earth's surface forever. —You children: one *present* thing
truly grasped would count for so many!
The whole of destiny crowds into childhood;
how often you would overtake your lover, panting,
panting from the blissful chase, aimless, breaking into freedom.

Life here is magic. Even *you* knew that, you girls
who seemed deprived of it, who were trapped in the city's
vilest streets, festering there, or cast aside
for rubbish. For each of you there was an hour, perhaps
not even a full hour, but between two intervals
a space not marked by the measures of time—,
when you had an *existence*. Everything. Veins filled with existence.
But we so easily forget what our laughing neighbor
neither covets nor confirms. We want to lift it up
and show it, even though the most visible happiness
only reveals itself when we've transformed it, within.

Nowhere, Love, will World exist but within. Our lives
pass in transformation. And all the while the outside realm
diminishes. Where once a solid house endured,
some abstraction shoves itself into view, completely at ease
among concepts, as if it still stood in the brain.
The Zeitgeist is building vast reservoirs of power, formless
as the thrusting energy it wrests from everything.
It no longer recognizes temples. Furtively we hoard
what the heart once lavished. Where one of them still survives,
an object once prayed to, revered, knelt before—,
it's already reaching, secretly, into the invisible world.
Many no longer see it, yet without the gain
of rebuilding it greater now, with pillars and statues, *within*!

Jede dumpfe Umkehr der Welt hat solche Enterbte,
denen das Frühere nicht und noch nicht das Nächste gehört.
Denn auch das Nächste ist weit für die Menschen. *Uns* soll
dies nicht verwirren; es stärke in uns die Bewahrung
der noch erkannten Gestalt.—Dies *stand* einmal unter Menschen,
mitten im Schicksal stands, im vernichtenden, mitten
im Nichtwissen-Wohin stand es, wie seiend, und bog
Sterne zu sich aus gesicherten Himmeln. Engel,
dir noch zeig ich es, *da!* in deinem Anschaun
steh es gerettet zuletzt, nun endlich aufrecht.
Säulen, Pylone, der Sphinx, das strebende Stemmen,
grau aus vergehender Stadt oder aus fremder, des Doms.

War es nicht Wunder? O staune, Engel, denn *wir* sinds,
wir, o du Großer, erzähls, daß wir solches vermochten, mein Atem
reicht für die Rühmung nicht aus. So haben wir dennoch
nicht die Räume versäumt, diese gewährenden, diese
unseren Räume. (Was müssen sie fürchterlich groß sein,
da sie Jahrtausende nicht unseres Fühlns überfülln.)
Aber ein Turm war groß, nicht wahr? O Engel, er war es,—
groß, auch noch neben dir? Chartres war groß—, und Musik
reichte noch weiter hinan und überstieg uns. Doch selbst nur
eine Liebende—, oh, allein am nächtlichen Fenster . . . .
reichte sie dir nicht ans Knie—?

                         Glaub *nicht*, daß ich werbe.
Engel, und würb ich dich auch! Du kommst nicht. Denn mein
Anruf ist immer voll Hinweg; wider so starke
Strömung kannst du nicht schreiten. Wie ein gestreckter
Arm ist mein Rufen. Und seine zum Greifen
oben offene Hand bleibt vor dir
offen, wie Abwehr und Warnung,
Unfaßlicher, weitauf.

Each dull turn of the world leaves such disinherited,
to whom neither the past nor the coming life lends substance.
For to humans even what comes next lies far away.
This ought not baffle us but strengthen our defense
of a still recognized form. —This once *stood* amidst men,
stood amidst Fate, the destroyer, stood
amidst Not-Knowing-Whither, as if it were alive there,
and arched stars closer from safeguarded heavens.
Angel, now *you* shall see it, too—*there!* In your gaze
it stands secured at last, erect for eternity.
Pillars, pylons, the Sphinx, the cathedral's
gray upward striving from a vanishing or alien city.

Miracles! O stand in wonder, Angel, for it was *us*,
O great one, *us*, tell the others of these things we added: my breath
is insufficient for such praise. So then we *haven't*
failed these generous spaces——, these spaces
that are *ours*. (How frighteningly vast they must be,
after millennia of our feelings not overflowing.)
But one tower was great, was it not? O Angel, it was,—
even next to you. Chartres was great—, and music
rose still higher, soared beyond us. But even
just one woman in love, alone, at night, at her window . . .
didn't she reach your knee—?
                                        Don't think I'm wooing.
Angel, and even if I were—you wouldn't come. For my
appeal is always full of "Away!" Against
so strong a current you cannot advance. My call is like
an outstretched arm. And its raised hand, tensed
as for grasping, remains before you
always, defense and warning,
Ungraspable One—palm out, wide open.

DIE ACHTE ELEGIE

Rudolf Kassner zugeeignet

Mit allen Augen sieht die Kreatur
das Offene. Nur unsre Augen sind
wie umgekehrt und ganz um sie gestellt
als Fallen, rings um ihren freien Ausgang.
Was draußen *ist*, wir wissens aus des Tiers
Antlitz allein; denn schon das frühe Kind
wenden wir um und zwingens, daß es rückwärts
Gestaltung sehe, nicht das Offne, das
im Tiergesicht so tief ist. Frei von Tod.
Ihn sehen wir allein; das freie Tier
hat seinen Untergang stets hinter sich
und vor sich Gott, und wenn es geht, so gehts
in Ewigkeit, so wie die Brunnen gehen.

Wir haben nie, nicht einen einzigen Tag,
den reinen Raum vor uns, in den die Blumen
unendlich aufgehn. Immer ist es Welt
und niemals Nirgends ohne Nicht: das Reine,
Unüberwachte, das man atmet und
unendlich *weiß* und nicht begehrt. Als Kind
verliert sich eins im Stilln an dies und wird
gerüttelt. Oder jener stirbt und *ists*.
Denn nah am Tod sieht man den Tod nicht mehr
und starrt *hinaus*, vielleicht mit großem Tierblick.
Liebende, wäre nicht der andre, der
die Sicht verstellt, sind nah daran und staunen . . .
Wie aus Versehn ist ihnen aufgetan
hinter dem andern . . . Aber über ihn
kommt keiner fort, und wieder wird ihm Welt.
Der Schöpfung immer zugewendet, sehn
wir nur auf ihr die Spiegelung des Frein,

THE EIGHTH ELEGY

Dedicated to Rudolf Kassner

With all its eyes the animal world
beholds the Open. Only our eyes
are as if inverted and set all around it
like traps at its portals to freedom.
What's outside we only know from the animal's
countenance; for almost from the first we take a child
and twist him round and force him to gaze
backwards and take in structure, not the Open
that lies so deep in an animal's face. Free from death.
Only *we* see death; the free animal has its demise
perpetually behind it and before it always
God, and when it moves, it moves into eternity,
the way brooks and running springs move.
   We, though: never, not for a single day, do we
have that pure space ahead of us into which flowers
endlessly open. What we have is World
and always World and never Nowhere-Without-Not:
that pure unguarded element one breathes
and *knows* endlessly and never craves. As a child
one gets lost there in the quiet, only to be
jostled back. Or someone dying *is* it.
For close to death one sees death no longer
and stares *out* instead, perhaps with the wide gaze of animals.
Lovers (were not the loved one there,
obstructing the view) draw near it and marvel . . .
Beyond the loved one, as if by accident,
the realm is glimpsed . . . But no one
gets beyond the other, and so World returns again.
Always turned so fervently toward creation,
we see only the reflection of the Open,

von uns verdunkelt. Oder daß ein Tier,
ein stummes, aufschaut, ruhig durch uns durch.
Dieses heißt Schicksal: gegenüber sein
und nichts als das und immer gegenüber.

Wäre Bewußtheit unsrer Art in dem
sicheren Tier, das uns entgegenzieht
in anderer Richtung—, riß es uns herum
mit seinem Wandel. Doch sein Sein ist ihm
unendlich, ungefaßt und ohne Blick
auf seinen Zustand, rein, so wie sein Ausblick.
Und wo wir Zukunft sehn, dort sieht es Alles
und sich in Allem und geheilt für immer.

Und doch ist in dem wachsam warmen Tier
Gewicht und Sorge einer großen Schwermut.
Denn ihm auch haftet immer an, was uns
oft überwältigt,—die Erinnerung,
als sei schon einmal das, wonach man drängt,
näher gewesen, treuer und sein Anschluß
unendlich zärtlich. Hier ist alles Abstand,
und dort wars Atem. Nach der ersten Heimat
ist ihm die zweite zwitterig und windig.
   O Seligkeit der *kleinen* Kreatur,
die immer *bleibt* im Schooße, der sie austrug;
o Glück der Mücke, die noch *innen* hüpft,
selbst wenn sie Hochzeit hat: denn Schooß ist Alles.
Und sieh die halbe Sicherheit des Vogels,
der beinah beides weiß aus seinem Ursprung,
als wär er eine Seele der Etrusker,
aus einem Toten, den ein Raum empfing,
doch mit der ruhenden Figur als Deckel.
Und wie bestürzt ist eins, das fliegen muß
und stammt aus einem Schooß. Wie vor sich selbst

which our own presence darkens. Or sometimes
a mute animal looks up and stares straight through us.
That's what destiny is: being opposite
and nothing else but that and always opposite.

If the assured animal that approaches us
on such a different path had in it consciousness
like ours—, it would wheel us round
and make us change our lives. But its existence
is for it infinite, ungrasped, completely
without reflection—, pure, like its outward gaze.
And where we see Future it sees Everything
and itself in Everything and healed forever.

And yet, upon that warm, alert animal
is the weight and care of an enormous sadness.
For what sometimes overwhelms us always
clings to it, too—a kind of memory that tells us
that what we're now striving for was once
nearer and truer and attached to us
with infinite tenderness. Here all is distance,
there it was breath. After the first home
the second one seems draughty and strangely sexed.
    O bliss of the *tiny* creatures, that live
their whole lives in the womb that brought them forth!
O joy of the gnat, which still leaps *within*,
even when it weds: for womb is all!
And look at the half-assurance of the bird,
from the manner of its birth almost knowing both worlds—
as if it were the soul of an Etruscan, released
from a dead man sealed in a space
that has his reclining figure for a lid.
And how confused is any womb-born creature
that has to fly! As if frightened

erschreckt, durchzuckts die Luft, wie wenn ein Sprung
durch eine Tasse geht. So reißt die Spur
der Fledermaus durchs Porzellan des Abends.

Und wir: Zuschauer, immer, überall,
dem allen zugewandt und nie hinaus!
Uns überfüllts. Wir ordnens. Es zerfällt.
Wir ordnens wieder und zerfallen selbst.

Wer hat uns also umgedreht, daß wir,
was wir auch tun, in jener Haltung sind
von einem, welcher fortgeht? Wie er auf
dem letzten Hügel, der ihm ganz sein Tal
noch einmal zeigt, sich wendet, anhält, weilt—,
so leben wir und nehmen immer Abschied.

of its own self, it zigzags through the air
like a crack through a teacup. The way a bat's trace
crazes the porcelain of evening.

And we: Spectators, always, everywhere,
looking at, never out of, everything!
It overfills us. We arrange it. It falls apart.
We rearrange it, and fall apart ourselves.

Who has turned us around like this, so that
always, no matter what we do, we're in the stance
of someone just departing? As he,
on the last hill that shows him all his valley
one last time, turns, stops, lingers—,
we live our lives, forever taking leave.

Warum, wenn es angeht, also die Frist des Daseins
hinzubringen, als Lorbeer, ein wenig dunkler als alles
andere Grün, mit kleinen Wellen an jedem
Blattrand (wie eines Windes Lächeln)—: warum dann
Menschliches müssen—und, Schicksal vermeidend,
sich sehnen nach Schicksal? . . .

                              Oh, *nicht*, weil Glück *ist*,
dieser voreilige Vorteil eines nahen Verlusts.
Nicht aus Neugier, oder zur Übung des Herzens,
das auch im Lorbeer *wäre* . . . . .

Aber weil Hiersein viel ist, und weil uns scheinbar
alles das Hiesige braucht, dieses Schwindende, das
seltsam uns angeht. Uns, die Schwindendsten. *Ein* Mal
jedes, nur *ein* Mal. *Ein* Mal und nichtmehr. Und wir auch
ein Mal. Nie wieder. Aber dieses
ein Mal gewesen zu sein, wenn auch nur *ein* Mal:
irdisch gewesen zu sein, scheint nicht widerrufbar.

Und so drängen wir uns und wollen es leisten,
wollens enthalten in unsern einfachen Händen,
im überfüllteren Blick und im sprachlosen Herzen.
Wollen es werden.—Wem es geben? Am liebsten
alles behalten für immer . . . Ach, in den andern Bezug,
wehe, was nimmt man hinüber? Nicht das Anschaun, das hier
langsam erlernte, und kein hier Ereignetes. Keins.
Also die Schmerzen. Also vor allem das Schwersein,
also der Liebe lange Erfahrung,—also
lauter Unsägliches. Aber später,

Why, when this span of life might be passed
as a laurel, slightly darker than everything else
green, with tiny waves on the edges
of each leaf (like the wind's smile)—: why then
have to be human—and, fleeing destiny,
long for destiny? . . .

                       Oh, *not* for some dream of happiness,
that premature profit of an imminent loss.
Not out of curiosity, not to give practice to the heart,
which would also pulse with laurel . . . . .

But because *life* here compels us, and because everything here
seems to need us, all this fleetingness
that strangely entreats us. Us, the *most* fleeting . . .
Once for each thing, only once. Once and no more. And we, too,
only once. Never again. But to have been
once, even though only once:
this having been *earthly* seems lasting, beyond repeal.

And so we press on and try to achieve it,
try to contain it in our simple hands,
in our brimming eyes, our voiceless heart.
Try to *become* it. Try to give it—to whom? Best of all,
to hold on to it all forever . . . Ah, but what can one carry across
into that other relation? Not the art of seeing,
learned so slowly here, and no event that transpired here. Not one.
The pain, then. Above all, the hard labor of living,
the long experience of love, —all the purely
unsayable things. But later on,

unter den Sternen, was solls: *die* sind *besser* unsäglich.
Bringt doch der Wanderer auch vom Hange des Bergrands
nicht eine Hand voll Erde ins Tal, die Allen unsägliche, sondern
ein erworbenes Wort, reines, den gelben und blaun
Enzian. Sind wir vielleicht *hier*, um zu sagen: Haus,
Brücke, Brunnen, Tor, Krug, Obstbaum, Fenster,—
höchstens: Säule, Turm . . . . aber zu *sagen*, verstehs,
oh zu sagen *so*, wie selber die Dinge niemals
innig meinten zu sein. Ist nicht die heimliche List
dieser verschwiegenen Erde, wenn sie die Liebenden drängt,
daß sich in ihrem Gefühl jedes und jedes entzückt?
Schwelle: was ists für zwei
Liebende, daß sie die eigne ältere Schwelle der Tür
ein wenig verbrauchen, auch sie, nach den vielen vorher
und vor den Künftigen . . . ., leicht.

Hier ist des *Säglichen* Zeit, *hier* seine Heimat.
Sprich und bekenn. Mehr als je
fallen die Dinge dahin, die erlebbaren, denn,
was sie verdrängend ersetzt, ist ein Tun ohne Bild.
Tun unter Krusten, die willig zerspringen, sobald
innen das Handeln entwächst und sich anders begrenzt.
Zwischen den Hämmern besteht
unser Herz, wie die Zunge
zwischen den Zähnen, die doch,
dennoch, die preisende bleibt.

Preise dem Engel die Welt, nicht die unsägliche, *ihm*
kannst du nicht großtun mit herrlich Erfühltem; im Weltall,
wo er fühlender fühlt, bist du ein Neuling. Drum zeig
ihm das Einfache, das, von Geschlecht zu Geschlechtern gestaltet,
als ein Unsriges lebt, neben der Hand und im Blick.
Sag ihm die Dinge. Er wird staunender stehn; wie du standest
bei dem Seiler in Rom, oder beim Töpfer am Nil.

among the stars, what then: there the unsayable *reigns*.
The traveler doesn't bring from the mountain slope
into the valley some handful of sod, around which all stand mute,
but a word he's gained, a pure word, the yellow and blue
gentian. What if we're here just for saying: *house*,
bridge, fountain, gate, jug, fruit tree, window,—
at most: *column, tower* . . . but for *saying*, understand,
oh for such saying as the things themselves
never hoped so intensely to be. Isn't this the sly purpose
of the taciturn earth, when it urges lovers on:
that in their passion each single thing should find ecstasy?
O Threshold: what must it mean for two lovers
to have their own older threshold and be wearing down so lightly
the ancient sill—, they too, after the many before,
before the many to come . . . . .

Here is the time for the sayable, *here* is its home.
Speak and attest. More than ever
the things we can live with are falling away,
and ousting them, filling their place: a will with no image.
Will beneath crusts which readily crack
whenever the act inside swells and seeks new borders.
Between the hammers our heart
lives on, as the tongue,
even between the teeth, remains
unceasing in praise.

Praise the world to the Angel, not what's unsayable.
You can't impress him with lofty emotions; in the cosmos
that shapes *his* feelings, you're a mere novice. Therefore show him
some simple object, formed from generation to generation
until it's truly our own, dwelling near our hands and in our eyes.
Tell him of *things*. He'll stand more amazed; as you stood
beside the ropemaker in Rome or by the potter along the Nile.

Zeig ihm, wie glücklich ein Ding sein kann, wie schuldlos und unser,
wie selbst das klagende Leid rein zur Gestalt sich entschließt,
dient als ein Ding, oder stirbt in ein Ding—, und jenseits
selig der Geige entgeht.—Und diese, von Hingang
lebenden Dinge verstehn, daß du sie rühmst; vergänglich,
traun sie ein Rettendes uns, den Vergänglichsten, zu.
Wollen, wir sollen sie ganz im unsichtbarn Herzen verwandeln
in—o unendlich—in uns! Wer wir am Ende auch seien.

Erde, ist es nicht dies, was du willst: *unsichtbar*
in uns erstehn?—Ist es dein Traum nicht,
einmal unsichtbar zu sein?—Erde! unsichtbar!
Was, wenn Verwandlung nicht, ist dein drängender Auftrag?
Erde, du liebe, ich will. Oh glaub, es bedürfte
nicht deiner Frühlinge mehr, mich dir zu gewinnen—, *einer*,
ach, ein einziger ist schon dem Blute zu viel.
Namenlos bin ich zu dir entschlossen, von weit her.
Immer warst du im Recht, und dein heiliger Einfall
ist der vertrauliche Tod.

Siehe, ich lebe. Woraus? Weder Kindheit noch Zukunft
werden weniger . . . . . Überzähliges Dasein
entspringt mir im Herzen.

Show him how happy a thing can be, how innocent and ours,
how even sorrow's lament resolves upon form,
serves as a thing or dies into a thing—, and in that blissful beyond
is unmoved even by the violin. —And these things
that keep alive on departure know that you praise them; transient,
they look to us, the *most* transient, to be their rescue.
They want us to change them completely, in our invisible hearts,
into—O endlessly—*us*! Whoever, finally, we may be.

Earth, isn't that what you want: to arise
in us *invisibly*? Isn't it your dream
to be invisible someday? Earth! Invisible!
What, if not transformation, is your urgent charge?
Earth, my darling, I will! Believe me, you need
no more of your springtimes to win me—, *one*,
just a single one, is already too much for my blood.
Nameless now, I am betrothed to you forever.
You've always been right, and your most sacred tenet
is Death the intimate Friend.

Look, I am living. On what? Neither childhood nor future
lessens . . . . . Superabundant existence
wells in my heart.

Daß ich dereinst, an dem Ausgang der grimmigen Einsicht,
Jubel und Ruhm aufsinge zustimmenden Engeln.
Daß von den klar geschlagenen Hämmern des Herzens
keiner versage an weichen, zweifelnden oder
reißenden Saiten. Daß mich mein strömendes Antlitz
glänzender mache; daß das unscheinbare Weinen
blühe. O wie werdet ihr dann, Nächte, mir lieb sein,
gehärmte. Daß ich euch knieender nicht, untröstliche Schwestern,
hinnahm, nicht in euer gelöstes
Haar mich gelöster ergab. Wir, Vergeuder der Schmerzen.
Wie wir sie absehn voraus, in die traurige Dauer,
ob sie nicht enden vielleicht. Sie aber sind ja
unser winterwähriges Laub, unser dunkeles Sinngrün,
eine der Zeiten des heimlichen Jahres—, nicht nur
Zeit—, sind Stelle, Siedelung, Lager, Boden, Wohnort.

Freilich, wehe, wie fremd sind die Gassen der Leid-Stadt,
wo in der falschen, aus Übertönung gemachten
Stille, stark, aus der Gußform des Leeren der Ausguß
prahlt: der vergoldete Lärm, das platzende Denkmal.
O, wie spurlos zerträte ein Engel ihnen den Trostmarkt,
den die Kirche begrenzt, ihre fertig gekaufte:
reinlich und zu und enttäuscht wie ein Postamt am Sonntag.
Draußen aber kräuseln sich immer die Ränder von Jahrmarkt.
Schaukeln der Freiheit! Taucher und Gaukler des Eifers!
Und des behübschten Glücks figürliche Schießstatt,
wo es zappelt von Ziel und sich blechern benimmt,
wenn ein Geschickterer trifft. Von Beifall zu Zufall
taumelt er weiter; denn Buden jeglicher Neugier
werben, trommeln und plärrn. Für Erwachsene aber

Someday, at the end of the nightmare of knowing,
may I emerge singing praise and jubilation to assenting angels.
May I strike my heart's keys clearly, and may none fail
because of slack, uncertain, or fraying strings.
May the tears that stream down my face
make me more radiant: may my hidden weeping
bloom. How I will cherish you then, you grief-torn nights!
Had I only received you, inconsolable sisters,
on more abject knees, only buried myself with more abandon
in your loosened hair. How we waste our afflictions!
We study them, stare out beyond them into bleak continuance,
hoping to glimpse some end. Whereas they're really
our wintering foliage, our dark greens of meaning, *one*
of the seasons of the clandestine year—; not only
a season—: they're site, settlement, shelter, soil, abode.

Ah, but the City of Pain: how strange its streets are:
the false silence of sound drowning sound,
and there—proud, brazen, effluence from the mold of emptiness—
the gilded hubbub, the bursting monument.
How an Angel would stamp out their market of solaces,
set up alongside their church bought to order:
clean and closed and woeful as a post office on Sunday.
Outside, though, there's always the billowing edge of the fair.
Swings of Freedom! High-divers and Jugglers of Zeal!
And the shooting gallery with its figures of idiot Happiness
which jump, quiver, and fall with a tinny ring
whenever some better marksman scores. Onward he lurches from cheers
to chance; for booths courting each curious taste
are drumming and barking. And then—for adults only—

ist noch besonders zu sehn, wie das Geld sich vermehrt, anatomisch,
nicht zur Belustigung nur: der Geschlechtsteil des Gelds,
alles, das Ganze, der Vorgang——, das unterrichtet und macht
fruchtbar . . . .
. . . . Oh aber gleich darüber hinaus,
hinter der letzten Planke, beklebt mit Plakaten des ›Todlos‹,
jenes bitteren Biers, das den Trinkenden süß scheint,
wenn sie immer dazu frische Zerstreuungen kaun . . . ,
gleich im Rücken der Planke, gleich dahinter, ists *wirklich*.
Kinder spielen, und Liebende halten einander,——abseits,
ernst, im ärmlichen Gras, und Hunde haben Natur.
Weiter noch zieht es den Jüngling; vielleicht, daß er eine junge
Klage liebt . . . . . Hinter ihr her kommt er in Wiesen. Sie sagt:
——Weit. Wir wohnen dort draußen . . . .

                       Wo? Und der Jüngling
folgt. Ihn rührt ihre Haltung. Die Schulter, der Hals——, vielleicht
ist sie von herrlicher Herkunft. Aber er läßt sie, kehrt um,
wendet sich, winkt . . . Was solls? Sie ist eine Klage.

Nur die jungen Toten, im ersten Zustand
zeitlosen Gleichmuts, dem der Entwöhnung,
folgen ihr liebend. Mädchen
wartet sie ab und befreundet sie. Zeigt ihnen leise,
was sie an sich hat. Perlen des Leids und die feinen
Schleier der Duldung.——Mit Jünglingen geht sie
schweigend.

Aber dort, wo sie wohnen, im Tal, der Älteren eine, der Klagen,
nimmt sich des Jünglinges an, wenn er fragt:——Wir waren,
sagt sie, ein Großes Geschlecht, einmal, wir Klagen. Die Väter
trieben den Bergbau dort in dem großen Gebirg; bei Menschen
findest du manchmal ein Stück geschliffenes Ur-Leid
oder, aus altem Vulkan, schlackig versteinerten Zorn.
Ja, das stammte von dort. Einst waren wir reich.——

a special show: how money breeds, its anatomy, not some charade:
money's genitals, everything, the whole act
from beginning to end—educational and guaranteed to make you
virile . . . .
. . . . Oh, but just beyond that,
behind the last of the billboards, plastered with signs for "Deathless,"
that bitter beer which tastes sweet to those drinking it
as long as they have fresh distractions to chew . . . ,
just beyond those boards, just on the other side: things are *real.*
Children play, lovers hold each other, off in the shadows,
pensive, on the meager grass, while dogs obey nature.
The youth is drawn farther on; perhaps he's fallen in love
with a young Lament . . . . . He pursues her, enters meadowland. She says:
"It's a long way. We live out there . . ."
                                        Where? And the youth follows.
Something in her bearing stirs him. Her shoulders, neck—,
perhaps she's of noble descent. Still, he leaves her, turns around,
glances back, waves . . . What's the use? She's a Lament.

Only the youthful dead, in the first state
of timeless equanimity, the phase of the unburdening,
follow her with loving steps. The girls
she waits for and befriends. Gently lets them see
the things that adorn her. Pearls of grief and the delicate
veils of suffrance. —When with young men
she walks on in silence.

Later, though, in the valley where they live, an older one, one of the elder
        Laments,
adopts the youth when he asks questions: —Long ago,
she says, we Laments were a powerful race. Our forefathers
worked the mines in those giant mountains; among humans
sometimes you'll find a fragment of polished primeval grief,
or, from an old volcano, a slag of petrified wrath.
Yes, it came from here. We used to be rich.—

Und sie leitet ihn leicht durch die weite Landschaft der Klagen,
zeigt ihm die Säulen der Tempel oder die Trümmer
jener Burgen, von wo Klage-Fürsten das Land
einstens weise beherrscht. Zeigt ihm die hohen
Tränenbäume und Felder blühender Wehmut,
(Lebendige kennen sie nur als sanftes Blattwerk);
zeigt ihm die Tiere der Trauer, weidend,—und manchmal
schreckt ein Vogel und zieht, flach ihnen fliegend durchs Aufschaun,
weithin das schriftliche Bild seines vereinsamten Schreis.—
Abends führt sie ihn hin zu den Gräbern der Alten
aus dem Klage-Geschlecht, den Sibyllen und Warn-Herrn.
Naht aber Nacht, so wandeln sie leiser, und bald
mondets empor, das über Alles
wachende Grab-Mal. Brüderlich jenem am Nil,
der erhabene Sphinx—: der verschwiegenen Kammer
Antlitz.
Und sie staunen dem krönlichen Haupt, das für immer,
schweigend, der Menschen Gesicht
auf die Waage der Sterne gelegt.

Nicht erfaßt es sein Blick, im Frühtod
schwindelnd. Aber ihr Schaun,
hinter dem Pschent-Rand hervor, scheucht es die Eule. Und sie,
streifend im langsamen Abstrich die Wange entlang,
jene der reifesten Rundung,
zeichnet weich in das neue
Totengehör, über ein doppelt
aufgeschlagenes Blatt, den unbeschreiblichen Umriß.

Und höher, die Sterne. Neue. Die Sterne des Leidlands.
Langsam nennt sie die Klage:—Hier,
siehe: den *Reiter*, den *Stab*, und das vollere Sternbild
nennen sie: *Fruchtkranz*. Dann, weiter, dem Pol zu:
Wiege; *Weg*; *Das Brennende Buch*; *Puppe*; *Fenster*.

And she guides him quietly through the wide landscape of Laments,
shows him the columns of temples, or the ruins
of those strongholds from which, long ago, Lament-Kings
wisely governed the land. Shows him the tall
trees of tears and the fields of flowering melancholy
(the living know them only as tender leaves):
shows him the animals of sorrow, grazing, —and sometimes
a bird startles, flies low through their lifted gazes, extends
into the distance the ancient glyph of its desolate cry.—
At evening she leads him out to the ancestral tombs
of the House of Lament, those of the sybils and the dire prophets.
But as night approaches, they move more slowly, until
suddenly, rising up moon-like, there appears: the great sepulchre
that watches over everything. Twin brother
to the one on the Nile, the exalted Sphinx—: visage
of the hidden chamber.
And they marvel at that kingly head, which silently,
for all time, has weighed the human face
in the stars' balance.

His sight can't grasp it, still unsteady
from recent death. But their gazing
flushes an owl out from behind the corona's rim. And the bird,
gliding with slow downstrokes along the cheek,
the one with the fullest curve,
inscribes faintly in the dead youth's new
sense of hearing, as across a doubly
unfolded page, the indescribable outline.

And higher, the stars. New ones. The stars of the Land of Pain.
Slowly the Lament names them: "There, look—
the *Rider*, the *Staff*, and that constellation with so many stars
they call: *Calyx*. And then farther, toward the pole:
Cradle; *Path*; *Puppet*; *Window*; *The Burning Book*.

Aber im südlichen Himmel, rein wie im Innern
einer gesegneten Hand, das klar erglänzende ›M‹,
das die Mütter bedeutet . . . . . . —

Doch der Tote muß fort, und schweigend bringt ihn die ältere
Klage bis an die Talschlucht,
wo es schimmert im Mondschein:
die Quelle der Freude. In Ehrfurcht
nennt sie sie, sagt:—Bei den Menschen
ist sie ein tragender Strom.—

Stehn am Fuß des Gebirgs,
Und da umarmt sie ihn, weinend.

Einsam steigt er dahin, in die Berge des Ur-Leids.
Und nicht einmal sein Schritt klingt aus dem tonlosen Los.

Aber erweckten sie uns, die unendlich Toten, ein Gleichnis,
siehe, sie zeigten vielleicht auf die Kätzchen der leeren
Hasel, die hängenden, oder
meinten den Regen, der fällt auf dunkles Erdreich im Frühjahr.—

Und wir, die an *steigendes* Glück
denken, empfänden die Rührung,
die uns beinah bestürzt,
wenn ein Glückliches *fällt*.

But in the southern sky, pure as if held in the palm
of a sacred hand: that clear, gleaming *M*
that means Mothers . . . . . ."

But the dead youth must go on, and the elder Lament
leads him in silence as far as the wide ravine,
where they see shimmering in moonlight:
the Font of Joy. She names it
reverently, saying, "Among the living
it becomes a powerful stream."

They stand at the foot of the range.
And she embraces him there, weeping.

He climbs on alone, into the mountains of primeval grief.
And no step rings back from that soundless fate.

But suppose the endlessly dead were to wake in us some emblem:
they might point to the catkins hanging
from the empty hazel trees, or direct us to the rain
descending on black earth in early spring.—

And we, who always think of happiness
rising, would feel the emotion
that almost baffles us
when a happy thing *falls*.

NOTES

women who loved: Many of the passages in the *Elegies* establish a shorthand, elliptical relationship to highly articulated figures in Rilke's imagination. About "women who love" Rilke wrote, just after completing "The First Elegy":

> I have no window on human beings. They give themselves to me only insofar as they make themselves heard within me, and during these last few years they have been communicating with me almost entirely through two forms, from which I infer things about human beings in general. What speaks to me of humanity, immensely, with a self-possessed calm that makes my hearing broad and spacious, is the phenomenon of the dead youth and, even more absolutely, purely, inexhaustibly: *the woman who loves.* In these two figures humanity gets stirred into my heart whether I want it to or not. They step forward on my stage with the clarity of the marionette (which is an outwardness entrusted with conviction) and, at the same time, as completed types, beyond which nothing can proceed, so that the natural history of their souls can be written.
>
> As for the woman who loves—I am not thinking of Saint Theresa and such grandiloquence as that—she gives herself to my attention much more distinctly, purely, i.e., undilutedly and (so to speak) unappliedly in the case of Gaspara Stampa, Louise Labé, certain Venetian courtesans, and, above all, Marianna Alcoforado [the "Portuguese Nun"], that incomparable creature, in whose eight weighty letters woman's love is for the first time traced from point to point, without ostentation, without exaggeration or mitigation, as if by the hand of a sibyl. And there, my God, there it becomes evident that, as a result of the inexorable logic of the female heart, this line was finished, perfected, not to be continued any further in the earthly realm, and could only be prolonged toward the divine, into infinity . . . Man, as a lover, was done with, finished with, *outloved*—if one may put it so circumspectly, outloved, as a glove is outworn . . . What a sad figure he plays in the history of love . . . How very much on one side, that of the woman, everything performed, endured, accomplished contrasts with man's absolute insufficiency in love.
>
> (To Annette Kolb, January 23, 1912)

Gaspara Stampa: An Italian noblewoman, Gaspara Stampa (1523–54) fell in love with Count Collatino di Collalto at the age of twenty-six and was deserted by him three years later. She responded by recording the story of their love and her experience of solitude and loss in a series of two hundred sonnets.

Santa Maria Formosa: A famous church in Venice, which Rilke visited twice in 1911. The reference is to one of the commemorative tablets on the church walls—it isn't known which one, though there has been much speculation.

Linos: An obscure figure of ancient Greek myth. Several legends refer to him, always in connection with music, early death, and his relation to Apollo—either as kin (brother, son) or slain, would-be rival. Some commentaries on "The First Elegy" cite stories in which the void left by Linos' death was so sudden and severe that its trembling amazement was called music. Others make reference to the ritual lament for Linos, supposedly related to music's origin because those who were numbed by his death were revived by the song of Orpheus. Whatever Rilke's sources (and they are fragmentary at best), he conflates the cosmological and the psychological to construct his own elliptical myth of grief: in the beginning plenitude, full space nurturing an "almost divine" youth; then fullness transformed into emptiness (the void is not originary here; it comes into being as the absence of presence) when the youth suddenly, inexplicably "steps out of it," "leaves," "is gone" (the word "death" is studiously avoided); then the penetration (equally inexplicable) of this absence—characterized not as a realm of lament but as shock petrifying into rigidity, numbness, an almost Golgotha-like aridity of feeling—by a music that is ambiguously both "first" and "adventuring" (the music is *already there*; no Orphic maker or source is indicated); so that the desert-spell is broken, the void comes alive—not with music per se but with "vibrations," phenomena prior to melodies heard or feelings felt. It is these same vibrations which "now" enrapture us, help us, and provide us solace.

vibrations: Compare Rilke's use of this term in his remarkable statement to his Polish translator about the whole of the *Elegies*:

> Nature, the things we move among and use, are provisional and perishable; but they are, for as long as we are here, *our* possession and our friendship, sharers in our trouble and our happiness, just as they were once the confidants of our ancestors. Therefore it is crucial not only that we not corrupt and degrade what constitutes the here and now, but, precisely because of the provisionality it shares with us, that these appearances and objects be comprehended by us in a most fervent understanding and transformed. Transformed? Yes, for our task is to stamp this provisional, perishing earth into ourselves so deeply, so painfully and passionately, that its being may rise again, "invisibly," in us. *We are the bees of the Invisible. Nous butinons éperdument le miel du visible, pour l'accumuler dans la grande ruche d'or de l'Invisible* [We wildly gather the honey of the visible, in order to store it in the great golden hive of the Invisible]. The *Elegies* show us at this work, this work of the continual conversion of the dear visible and tangible into the invisible vibration [*Schwingung*] and agitation of our nature, which introduces new vibration-numbers [*Schwingungszahlen*] into the vibration-spheres [*Schwingungs-Sphären*] of the universe. (For, since the various materials in the cosmos are only different vibration-rates [*Schwingungsexponenten*], we are preparing in this way, not only intensities of a spiritual kind, but—who knows?— new bodies, metals, nebulae, and constellations.)

(To Witold von Hulewicz, November 13, 1925)

Tobias: A figure from the Apocryphal book of Tobit. Ordered by his dying father to travel from Nineveh to Media to retrieve a sum of money being held for him there by another man, Tobias looks for someone who knows the way, and encounters a youth his own age who is the archangel Raphael in disguise. The angel agrees to accompany him, "and so the two went forth, and the young man's dog went with them."

Attic stelae: Ancient Greek marble tombstones or funerary plaques, often carved with scenes of intimate, everyday human interaction.

THE FOURTH ELEGY

the boy with the brown squint-eye: Rilke's cousin, Egon von Schiele (1873–80), to whose memory the eighth sonnet of the Second Part of the *Sonnets to Orpheus* is dedicated. Rilke wrote of him:

> I often think of him and keep on returning to his figure, which has remained for me indescribably affecting. Much "childhood," the sadness and helplessness of childhood, is embodied for me in his form, in the ruff he wore, in his neck, in his chin, in his beautiful brown eyes, disfigured by a squint. So I invoked him once more in connection with that eighth Sonnet, which expresses transitoriness, after he had already served as the prototype for little Erick Brahe, the dead child, in *The Notebooks of Malte Laurids Brigge*.
>
> (To Phia Rilke, January 24, 1924; in Carl Sieber,
> *René Rilke: Die Jugend Rainer Maria Rilke* [Leipzig, 1932], p. 59f.)

THE FIFTH ELEGY

Dedication: Frau Hertha Koening was a lyricist who in December 1914 had purchased, perhaps at Rilke's suggestion, Picasso's 1905 painting *La famille des saltimbanques*. Rilke subsequently wrote to her asking permission to reside in her Munich apartment while she was away on her country vacation. She granted his request, and he spent the summer and early fall of 1915 living beside "the great Picasso." The human figures who stand quietly, almost abstractedly in Picasso's painting do influence "The Fifth Elegy" (though as much in ontological mood as in detail), but they mingle in Rilke's imagination with a troupe of real-life acrobats he observed with fascination during his first years in Paris. ("And so now the 'Saltimbanques' too are there, who had such a profound impact on me during my earliest stay in Paris and who have been packed away inside me ever since," Rilke wrote to Lou Andreas-Salomé on February 20, 1922, just days after finishing "The Fifth Elegy.") These actual acrobats inspired an entry in one of

Rilke's notebooks dated July 14, 1907. Comparing it to Picasso's so differently haunting tableau may suggest something of the complex alchemy at work in "The Fifth Elegy":

In front of the Luxembourg Gardens, near the Panthéon, Père Rollin and his troupe have spread themselves out again. The same carpet lies there, the same thick winter overcoats have been removed and piled on top of a chair so that there is just enough room for the little boy, the old man's grandson, to come and sit down on its edge during breaks. He still needs to—he's a beginner, after all—and his feet hurt from those steep jumps out of high somersaults onto the ground. He has a large face that can hold a great many tears, and yet they often well up all the way to the edge of his widened eyes. Then he has to carry his head very cautiously, like an overfull cup. It's not that he's sad, not at all; he wouldn't even notice if he were. It's simply the pain that cries, and he has no choice but to let it cry. It will grow fainter with the passage of time and eventually disappear. The father has long since forgotten what it was like, and the grandfather, well, it's been sixty years since he forgot it, otherwise he wouldn't be so famous. But look, Père Rollin, who has become a legend at all the fairs, doesn't "work" anymore. He no longer lifts huge weights and he (once the most eloquent of all) says nothing now. He's been assigned the drum. Touchingly patient, he stands there with his long-gone athlete's face, whose features sag loosely into one another, as if a weight had been hung on each one and pulled it down. Dressed like a commoner, a knitted sky-blue tie around his colossal neck, he has withdrawn at the height of his fame into this coat and into this modest position upon which, so to speak, glory no longer falls. But any one of these young people who has ever seen him knows that in those sleeves are hidden the famous muscles whose slightest play would cause the weights to leap. That person has vivid memories of one such masterful performance, and he says a few words to his neighbor and points across, and then the old man feels their eyes on him, pensive and uncertain and respectful. That strength is still there, young people, he thinks; it's not as available as it used to be, that's all; it has descended into the roots; it's still there somewhere, all of it. And it's really far too much for just beating a drum. And he pounds away. But he pounds too rapidly. His son-in-law whistles over to him and signals him to stop; he was right in the middle of his spiel. The old man breaks off, frightened, and makes excuses with his heavy shoulders and shifts his weight ponderously onto his other leg. But already he has to be whistled off again. *Diable.* Père! Père Rollin! He's already started drumming again. He scarcely realizes it. He could drum on forever and ever, they mustn't think he'd get tired. But there, now his daughter is talking; sharp-witted and sturdy and solid and with more brains than the others. She now holds the thing together; it's a joy to watch her. The son-in-law does good work, no one can deny that, and he does it willingly, as if that's his function. But she has it in her blood, one can see that. It's something she was born to. She's ready: "*Musique!*" she shouts. And the old man drums away like fourteen drummers. "Père Rollin, hey, Père Rollin," calls one of the spectators, and steps right up, recognizing him. But he only gives him a slight nod; his drumming is a sacred trust, and he takes it with utmost seriousness.

that first capital letter: Commentators usually gloss this passage along the following lines: Rilke, perceiving the standing figures in the Picasso *Saltimbanques* as forming a large *D*, puns on this visual peculiarity by coining the word *Dastehen* (roughly, "standing-thereness," and strongly echoing *Dasein*—"existence," "being-thereness") to register the quality of the acrobats' presence. Hence the translator's challenge to find an equivalent word that begins with a capital *D*. But this line of thought may be fundamentally in error. The elegy visualizes a family of itinerant acrobats *performing* in the outlying regions of the city before passersby who randomly gather and disperse. The large capital letter of their *Dastehen*—barely there, only for a moment "erect" and "on show," before "even the strongest" are rolled and crumpled again— likely refers to the figure they construct in one of their feats of acrobatic balancing (later in the elegy Rilke will employ the metaphor of a swiftly erected and deconstructed tree). The capital letter they form would thus be like those in the "grotesque alphabets" of entwined bodies so popular with late medieval engravers. And assuming that the capital letter they form exists in some written alphabet (for *Dastehen*, after all, may spell itself differently), *D* seems an especially unlikely figure for an acrobatic tour-de-force to construct.

August the Strong: The reference is to August II, King of Poland (1670–1733). He was notorious for his feats of strength, his drinking bouts, and his sexual prowess. According to legend he fathered more than a hundred children.

"Subrisio Saltat": An abbreviation for *subrisio saltatoris*—"acrobat's smile." The passage envisions an apothecary's shelf with rows of small labeled vials on it.

THE SIXTH ELEGY

Karnak: The site of the Temple of Amon in southern Egypt, which Rilke visited in January 1911. The temple's stone pillars depict battle scenes with the pharaoh-generals in their conquering chariots.

THE EIGHTH ELEGY

Dedication: Rudolf Kassner (1873–1959) was an Austrian cultural philosopher and friend of Rilke's from 1907 to the very end of the latter's life. They admired each other greatly, but differed over key issues. Kassner argued (from the position of a philosophical, allegorized pseudo-Christianity) that the human limitations Rilke laments as tragic and inexplicable are in fact necessary conditions which a mature "conversion" must accept. He considered the latter's depiction of "the Open" and the animal's pure consciousness as "atavistic."

the soul of an Etruscan: The Etruscans depicted the soul as a bird on the walls of their sarcophagus-chambers. The lids of the sarcophagi themselves were often sculpted representations of the dead person lying in repose.

the corona's rim: Rilke's *Pschent* is the Arabic spelling of the Greek transcription of the ancient Egyptian word for the double crown worn by the pharaohs to signify the union of Upper and Lower Egypt. But turn-of-the-century Egyptologists also used the term to designate the royal headcloth over which the crown was worn. Before the restoration of the Sphinx in 1925, an actual owl supposedly nested at the headcloth's edge.